ActionScript 2.0
GARAGE

The Garage Series

Street-smart books about technology

Each author **presents** a unique take on solving problems, using a format designed to replicate the **experience** of Web searching.

Technology presented and **organized** by useful topic—not in a linear tutorial style.

Books that cover **whatever** needs to be covered to get the project done. Period.

Eben Hewitt, *Java Garage.* ISBN: 0321246233.
Tara Calishain, *Web Search Garage.* ISBN: 0131471481.
Kirk McElhearn, *iPod & iTunes Garage.* ISBN: 0131486454.
Marc Campbell, *Web Design Garage.* ISBN: 0131481991.
Don Jones, *PHP-Nuke Garage.* ISBN: 0131855166.
Dan Livingston, *ActionScript 2.0 Garage.* ISBN: 0131484753.

```
                        <a garage is where you work.
        in a garage, you do your  work, not somebody else's.
        it's where you experiment and listen to the old ball
                                      game. make music.
                                           get away.
                                            tinker.
        it's where you do projects for passion, make your own
                                            rules, and
                          plot like an evil genius./>
```

(Irreverent. **Culturally rooted.**)

Edgy and fun. Lively writing.
(The impersonal voice of an
omniscient narrator is not
allowed!)

[**Eben Hewitt,** series editor]

Check out the series at www.phptr.com/garageseries

ActionScript 2.0
GARAGE

Dan Livingston

Prentice Hall Professional Technical Reference

Upper Saddle River, NJ • Boston • Indianapolis
San Francisco • New York • Toronto • Montreal
London • Munich • Paris • Madrid • Copetown
Sydney • Tokyo • Singapore • Mexico City

PRENTICE
HALL
PTR

U. S. Corporate and Government Sales
(800) 382-3419
corpsales@pearsontechgroup.com

For sales outside the U. S., please contact:

International Sales
international@pearsoned.com

Visit us on the Web: www.phptr.com

Library of Congress Cataloging-in-Publication Data:

Livingston, Dan.
  ActionScript 2.0 garage / Dan Livingston.
    p. cm.
  ISBN 0-13-148475-3 (pbk. : alk. paper)
  1. Computer animation.   2. Flash (Computer file)   3. Web sites—Design.
  4. ActionScript (Computer program language)   I. Title.

TR897.7.L585 2005
006.7'8—dc22   2004025424

ISBN 0-13-148475-3

Text printed in the United States on recycled paper at Edwards Brothers in Ann Arbor Michigan.
Second printing, June 2005

To Annie,
the sassy Pirate Queen

Contents

Preface

Welcome to *ActionScript 2.0 Garage*. The goal of this book is to make learning ActionScript more fun. A lot more fun.

Okay, it's not a big dream, but it's *my* dream.

I'm not kidding. The goal of this book is to show beginning to intermediate ActionScript programmers how to take their skills to the next level and blast out some amazing code. The code samples in here are actual working chunks of code, not just-for-computer-books-but-no-one-would-EVER-use-this-in-the-real-world stuff.

That, and I attempted to have something of a (gasp) *personality* (shriek) while talking about code. I'm aiming for "helpful smart-alec" (or "chaotic good" if you're old-school).

Who This Book Is For

This book is for beginning to intermediate ActionScript programmers who want a quick, friendly way to get deeper into ActionScript code. If you don't know what **trace()** is, put this book down right now before you hurt somebody. I'm not kidding. Right now!

Who This Book Isn't For

Junkies. Heiresses. Shepherds. I make fun of George Lucas a few times, and maybe Orlando Bloom too—I can't remember for sure. (He was great in *Troy*, you know. He did a wonderful job in the role of Helen.)

What's in the Book

This book has everything from arrays to objects to how to manipulate components: Component skins. Styles. Functions. Best practices. Lots and lots of code and working examples. You can download everything from www.wire-man.com/garage.

What's Not in the Book

Data components don't really involve ActionScript, so I left them out. I don't cover advanced object-oriented anything or how to use the animation bits of the Flash program.

About the Attitude

You may notice this tome's tone is a little rougher than other computer books you've read. That's because we want this book to make learning *fun*, so we decided to spice it up a bit. If you go through the book and don't learn a thing about ActionScript, I hope you're at least a little entertained. (Update: I just got word that my editor has toned down the profanity and numerous pornography references, so perhaps it's a tad less entertaining now.)

What's New in AS2

assume you already know something about ActionScript and Flash. If you're a complete newbie with ActionScript, you should put this book down right now before you hurt yourself. I'm going to move at a brisk clip here.

Super-Short History

Real ActionScript appeared in Flash 5. It was improved in Flash MX and, for MX2004, changed enough so that it's now called ActionScript 2.0 (AS2 from here on out).

What Is AS2 Really?

AS2 is not a new language. It's a somewhat new syntax of an old language, ActionScript 1.0 (AS1). In fact, AS2 gets compiled in AS1 when it becomes an SWF file (SWF used to mean Shockwave File, but Macromedia says it now means Small Web File). ActionScript is supposed to be three to seven times faster than AS1. I haven't seen any tests to prove this claim, but it seems speedy enough for me.

Does AS1 Still Work?

Yep—your old code will still work in a Flash MX2004 movie. This can be handy because while AS2 is great for large projects, sometimes it's too much for little sites you have to create quickly. Using AS2 can feel like you're building a tank, but sometimes duct tape is all you need.

Biggest Change: New Class Syntax

Macromedia wants to make AS2 more enticing to real developers—people who program in Java and C++ and whatnot. To draw them in, the syntax to create classes and packages looks a lot more like Java.

Briefly, you create classes in separate files that contain class {...} structures, and you can create methods and properties that are public, private, and static. For (much) more on this, check out Topic 40, Classes and Objects: An Introduction.

Components

MX2004 has a whole new architecture for components called v2. Essentially, there are a lot more components, including several kinds of menus and some that deal with Web Services. Also, components are now compiled, which means the code is hidden from you (although by the time you read this, some decompilers will probably be floating around).

Some other new stuff:

- The listener event model allows listener objects to handle events (more in Topic 44, Events, Handlers, and Listeners).
- Skinning properties mean that you load states only when you need to.
- CSS-based styles let you create a separate style document that multiple movies can share (Topic 31, Stylesheets).
- Themes are sets of component graphics and behaviors you can slap onto a set of components (Topic 10, Setting Skins and Styles: Halo and Sample).
- A couple of manager classes allow you to more easily handle depth and focus.
- The classes `UIObject` and `UIcomponent` provide core functionality for all components. To really understand components, it's good to be familiar with what these classes do. (That's beyond the scope of this little book, though.)
- You can create extendable classes—components that are subclasses of existing components (Topic 42, Extending the Movie Clip Class).

General Changes

- All variable and keywords are case sensitive.

- If an undefined variable is used as a number, its default value is NaN (Not a Number). For example, with `trace(myNumber + 1);`, `myNumber` used to be 0; now it's NaN.

- If an undefined variable is used as a string, its default value is "undefined." It used to be an empty string ("").

- As long as strings aren't empty, they have a Boolean value of true.

Language Changes

Here's a brief summary of changes. I'll let you RTFM (read the, uh, fantastic manual) for the specific syntaxes and such.

- `Array.sort()` and `Array.sortOn()` allow extra sort parameters so you can set ascending or descending sorting order and consider case sensitivity.

- The `ContextMenu` and `ContentMenuItem` classes let you customize the menu that pops up when someone right-clicks (PC) or control-clicks (Mac). You can reach these properties via `Button.menu`, `MovieClip.menu`, and `Textfield.menu`.

- Error handling takes place through the `Error` class, `throw`, and `try...catch`—finally.

- You can use `LoadVars.addRequestHeader` and `XML.addRequestHeader` to tweak HTTP request headers.

- `MMExecute()` lets you execute Flash JavaScript API commands.

- AS2 offers better depth handling via `MovieClip.getNextHighestDepth()` and `MovieClip.getInstanceAtDepth()`. I'm happy to see these changes—my depths and levels often get a little out of control.

- `Movieclikp.getSWFVersion()` gets the Flash Player version of a loaded SWF file.

- `MovieClip.getTextSnapshot()` lets you work with static text in a movie clip. The only way to create static text is during authoring. All runtime text fields are either *dynamic* or *input*. Note that *runtime* means "created by ActionScript while the Flash movie is playing."

- `MovieClip._lockroot` lets you specify a movie clip that will act as _root for any movie clips loaded into it, or lets you specify that the meaning of _root in a movie clip won't change if it's loaded into a different movie clip.

- The `MovieClipLoader` class lets you monitor the progress of files as they're being loaded. Its purpose is to just watch the loading and report on it.

- The `NetStream` and `NetConnection` classes let you stream local video files (FLV files only).

- The `PrintJob` class gives you more control over printing.

- `Sound.onID3` gives you access to ID3 information in a sound file, if it exists. If it does, you can get to that property via the `Sound.id3` property (more in Topic 25, MP3s and ActionScript).

- More objects and methods are provided in the `System` class, and more methods are provided in `System.capabilities`.

- `TextField.condenseWhite` lets you remove extra white space from HTML text.

- `TextField.mouseWheelEnabled` lets you specify whether a text field scrolls when the user rolls the mouse wheel. You also get the `Mouse.onMouseWheel` event listener.

- The `TextField.StyleSheet` class lets you create a CSS-like style sheet object that can be used over and over. It also includes the `Textfield.styleSheet` property.

- `TextFormat.getTextExtent()` returns all sorts of super-precise information about a text field.

Strong Typing

I f you're from the scripting (JavaScript or ActionScript) world, you may not even know what a data type is or why you should care about one. Truthfully, you don't have to, but it'll help you become a better (or at least more thorough) programmer.

Variables have data types: strings, numbers, arrays, objects, Booleans, and so on. In AS1, you could make this assignment with no problem:

```
var template = "catalog";
trace(template);
template = 5;
trace(template);
```

The output would look like Figure 2.1.

In fact, this approach still works in MX2004. However, it's bad programming practice. Bad! (Repeat offenders should be forced to watch the even-numbered *Star Trek* movies, like *Star Trek VI: Undiscovered Country*, twice—man, that one was bad. The campfire scenes? Sheesh.) Generally, variables shouldn't change data type—it makes your code too confusing.

DO OR DIE:

> > Set what kind of value a variable can accept: string, number, array, and so on.

> > Throw an error if the wrong data tries to get in.

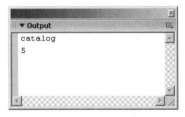

Figure 2.1
Swapping Data Types

Strong data typing looks like this:

```
var template:String = "catalog";
```

This code means that the template variable must be a string. If you try to make it anything else, Flash throws an error. For example, try this:

```
var template:String = "catalog";
trace(template);
template = 5;
trace(template);
```

You'll get Figure 2.2.

Whaddaya think will happen here?

```
var bar:Number;
var barNone = bar/2;
barNone = "bayToBreakers";
trace(barNone);
```

Will you get an error? Does **barNone** inherit the **Number** data type from bar? Test the movie, and you'll get the output shown in Figure 2.3.

No error. While **bar** is strongly typed as a number, **barNone** definitely isn't. If you want to make sure **barNone** stays a number, you must use this code:

```
var bar:Number;
var barNone:Number = bar/2;
barNone = "bayToBreakers";
trace(barNone);
```

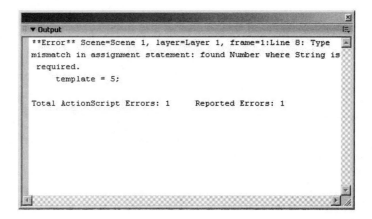

Figure 2.2

A Strong Data Type Exerting Itself

Test the movie now, and you'll get an error.

Yes, strong typing is something of a pain initially. However, it will most likely save you from yourself later, resulting in less pain overall. It's kind of like a flu shot.

BUT...

Don't be thick-headed about it by typing your variables no matter what. Sometimes, it's useful for your variables to be free and loose and whatever they feel like being. That's one of the advantages of a scripting language. Generally, I like to type my variables unless I have a reason not to (such as that I'm lazy).

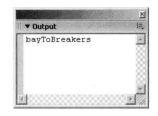

Figure 2.3

No Error—Strong Typing Isn't Inherited

Strong Typing and Code Hints

Strong typing can also help with code hints. When you're working in the Actions panel, you may notice that Flash can sometimes figure out what you're typing and give you options. (See Figure 2.4.)

If you strong-type a variable, then Flash knows what kind of methods your variable can now work with. For example, if you create a string, you can use indexOf(), split(), and toLowerCase(). (See Figure 2.5.)

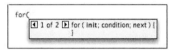

Figure 2.4

Flash Sometimes Offers Options

This isn't a huge deal, but it's convenient.

So, I hear you ask, what kinds of data types can I use? What's out there besides Array and String and Object? Oh, my, I say, a fantabulous plethora (actual English—silly, but correct).

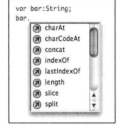

Figure 2.5

Flash Lists the Methods Available to the Variable

Accordion	DataHolder	Label
Alert	DataSet	List
Array	DataType	LoadVars
Binding	Date	LocalConnection
Button	DateChooser	Log
Camera	DateField	MediaController
Checkbox	Delta	MediaDisplay
Color	DeltaItem	MediaPlayback
ComboBox	DeltaPacket	Menu
ComponentMixins	EndPoint	MenuBar
CustomActions	Error	Microphone
DataGrid	Function	MovieClip

MovieClipLoader	RDBMSResovler	Tree
NetConnection	ScrollPane	TypedValue
NetStream	SharedObject	Void
Number	Slide	WebServiceConnector
NumericStepper	SOAPCall	Window
Object	Sound	XML
PendingCall	String	XMLConnector
PopUpManager	TextArea	XMLNode
PrintJob	TextField	XMLSocket
ProgressBar	TextFormat	XUpdateResolver
RadioButton	TextInput	
RadioButtonGroup	TextSnapshot	

If you're just being introduced to strong typing, chances are you'll use only a few of these. Most likely, you'll stick to Array, Color, Date, LoadVars, MovieClip, Number, Object, Sound, String, and XML. Don't be afraid to experiment, though.

More Ways to Get Those Precious Code Hints

You can end your variable name with a special suffix that tells Flash, "This is a String" or "This is an Object." Flash then displays the appropriate code hints for you. For example, the following causes code hints to appear. (See Figure 2.6.)

```
var warning_array = new Array();
warning_array.
```

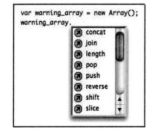

Figure 2.6

Flash Provides Code Hints

Note that this is *not* strong typing. It is just using a special variable name to make code hints appear. No errors will occur if you type in this code:

```
var warning_array = new Array();
warning_array = "hi there";
```

Also note that the following won't work:

```
var warning_array;
warning_array.
```

No code hints this way, buddy.

In some programming languages, strong typing allows the program to run faster. Not so in ActionScript: It doesn't affect performance even a little bit.

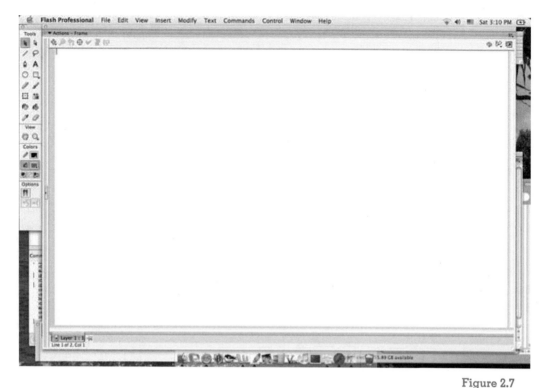

Figure 2.7

Big, Free-Floating Actions Panel

So What?

It's not that big a deal, really. If you already prefer to code in the Flash Actions panel, then the code hints can occasionally be helpful. If that's your preference, here's an easy way to work in the Actions panel:

1. Detach the Actions panel from the other panels so that it's free-floating.

2. Resize the panel until it's as big as you can make it, as in Figure 2.7.

3. Press F9, and the panel disappears. Press F9 again, and it's back.

   Give it a shot—see if you like programming this way. I kinda like it.

Tricking Flash

Not that you'd want to do this, but here's a way to get around strong typing:

```
var numTrees:Number = 5;
trace(numTrees);           // displays "5"
```

```
var treeHack = "numTrees";
this[treeHack] = "leafy green";   // no error happens
trace(numTrees);                  // displays "leafy green"
```

Why?

ActionScript is looking at an associative array (an associative array uses strings instead of numbers as an index, such as `myArray["ice"]` instead of `myArray[3]`), so it can't be sure what kind of value `treeHack` is. It's a variable, and variables can change, so Flash can't be sure what `treeHack` will be.

Function Return Typing

 unction return typing is a lot like strong typing. It looks like this:

```
function wardrobeMalfunction(numSnaps):Number
{
    // bunch of code here
    return numBoobsDisplay;
}
```

All this says is that numBoobsDisplay had better be a number, or Flash will throw an error. For example,

```
function wardrobeMalfunction(numSnaps):Number
{
    var revealed:String = "Go Justin go";
    return revealed;
}
wardrobeMalfunction(5);
```

results in an error because we tried to return a string when the function demands that a number be returned.

Here's another example that returns an array.

```
origArray = ["the
fonz","Bumblecakes","sea","DeeDee","Eek","fark","ghost","ha-cha-
cha","eye","Homer Jay"]

function shuffleArray(userArray):Array
{
    var tempArray:Array = new Array();
    var shuffledArray:Array = new Array();

    // create a copy
    for (i=0; i<userArray.length; i++) tempArray[i] = userArray[i];

    // create the shuffled array
    while (tempArray.length > 0) {
        randomElement = int(Math.random()*tempArray.length);
        shuffledArray.push(tempArray[randomElement]);
        tempArray.splice(randomElement,1);
    }
    return shuffledArray;
}

shuffled = shuffleArray(origArray);
trace (shuffled);
```

FAQ

Tom* Asks Why

As with strong typing, the idea is to force you to follow your own rules. You should know what your functions are returning, and you should know if they're doing something different. As with strong typing, it doesn't do anything but alert you to potential bugs in your code—and it builds muscles. Gives you a cute butt. So do it.

---

* I have a friend named Tom who recently gave computer programming the one-finger salute and returned to his musical roots. But while he was learning to program, he complained about computer books. "They tell you *how* to do something, but not *when* to do it!" So, in an effort to avoid the aforementioned salute, I'll try to add a little context to the code and let you know when to actually use a certain function or method.

On my Web site (www.wire-man.com/garage), you can download the code, which contains comments that talk a bit more about the code.

Try changing the bolded `Array` to `Number`, and see what happens. (That's right. The moon falls out of orbit.)

```
**Error** Scene=Scene 1, layer=Layer 1, frame=1:Line 17: The
expression returned must match the function's return type.
        return shuffledArray;


Total ActionScript Errors: 1     Reported Errors: 1
```

PART I

Forms

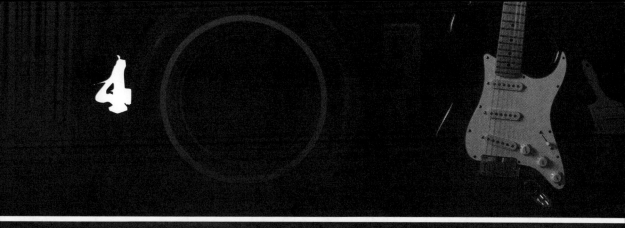

Forms: Flash or HTML?

he first question you should ask yourself when doing anything in Flash is, Why not HTML? HTML works in all browsers, doesn't require a plug-in, and loads faster. You can do a lot with DHTML and JavaScript. From a usability standpoint, people are far more used to seeing HTML form elements than Flash ones and are likely to be more comfortable using them.

Remember, Web sites are all about getting the users to their goals as soon and as easily as possible, not about having cool technology just for the sake of technology.

So, why bother with Flash?

- Validation: If you use Flash forms, you can guarantee client-side data validation. That is, you know you can check the user's input before you send it off to the server. You can't do that with HTML, since the user can turn off JavaScript.

- Smoother user experience (once movie is downloaded): If you have a lot of form elements, you can use ActionScript to quickly show and hide information—faster than HTML can make a round trip to the server and back to show a new HTML page.

- Cross-platform and cross-browser reliability: If the browser has the Flash plug-in, your interface will look the same in all browsers. (I use *interface* here instead *movie* because that's a more exact description of what we're building. This book cares less about animations and more about code that responds to what the user does.)

- More flexibility: You can do more with ActionScript in a Flash interface than you can with JavaScript in an HTML page.

Then, why skip Flash?

- The whole plug-in thing: You don't know which version of the Flash plug-in the user has. It's almost a guarantee that he or she has some version of it.
- Download size: SWFs take more kilobytes than HTML. For example, let's look at a simple form in Flash (Figure 4.1) and HTML (Figure 4.2).

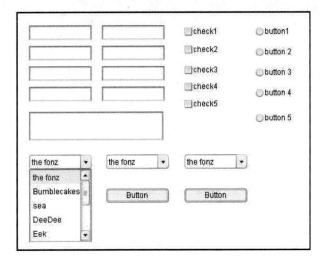

Figure 4.1

Form Elements Using UI Components

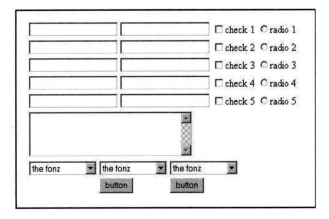

Figure 4.2

Regular HTML Form Elements

For the Flash page, I used the built-in components, which take up more memory. Pretty big difference: 62KB for the Flash file and only 2KB for HTML. The Flash one definitely looks nicer, though, and I put it together faster than the HTML (but I'm a hand-codin' fool, so using Dreamweaver or something would probably be as fast as using Flash).

So What to Do?

Think about what's best for the users. Users, users, users. Bless their daft little CD-tray-as-cup-holder hearts. Generally, my preference is to use HTML unless there's a pressing reason to use Flash. If the rest of the site's in Flash, then the user will already have to have the plug-in and have a fast enough pipe to handle the download times.

UNDER THE HOOD

That any given user has some version of the Flash plug-in is a near certainty because of two things: Macromedia says that 96 percent of all Web browsers have Flash installed. This may be true, but what really sells me is that for years, computers have come with browsers pre-installed, and the Flash plug-in has been part of that pre-installation. Since users can be counted on to be lazy (or to not care what a plug-in is or even what Flash is), they'll just use what their computers came with. If I remember right, Flash was being pre-installed by 1999, and chances are, most of your audience is using a computer purchased since then.

Creating a Form Using Components

his first little section covers what components are, so if you know that already, just blip over the next couple paragraphs.

DO OR DIE:

> > Add the component to the Library by dragging it to the Stage, then deleting it.

> > Place the component in your movie using `createClassObject()` or `attachMovie()`. It doesn't really matter which one you use.

What Are Components?

Components have been in Flash since Flash 5, when they were called Smart Clips. They're little self-contained movie clips, with frames, graphics, and scripting, all in a neat little package. In fact, in MX2004, components are compiled, which means that you can't take them apart to see how they tick (you could do this in Flash MX and see all the internal ActionScript, which is hidden by the compiling).

Drag a component to the Stage, and you can interact with it like any other movie clip. You can move it around, hide it, control it with ActionScript, and so on. Most components have their own little behaviors programmed in as well. For example, the ComboBox component (which looks like the HTML `<select>` form element) displays its menu items when you click on it. You don't have to code this item-showing behavior—it's already in the component. It just works. Components can be, well, anything a movie clip can be. You can get pretty

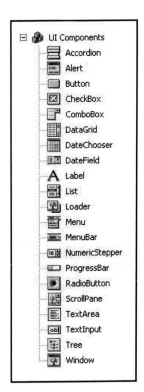

Figure 5.1

The UI Components

sophistimacated. The only way to really understand them is to start using them, so let's do that.

The form components are included in the gaggle of UI components that comes with MX04: input text fields, checkboxes, radio buttons, drop-down menus and the like (see Figure 5.1).

Being the brilliant AS-er that you are, you don't need to use a single one of these—you could create them all on your own, with your own graphics and ActionScript. But why bother? Mechanics don't build a new car every time they go on a road trip.

The easiest way to create a form using components is, predictably, to drag the little buggers onto your Stage. This works great if you know exactly what's going on your form—say, if you know you have to collect name, address, email, and credit card information.

However, if you're creating a dynamic form, and you won't know which form elements are needed until the user gives you some data, then you need to stay flexible. Let's do that.

Two Ways to Add Components

There are two ways to dynamically add components to your interface.

```
createClassObject()
attachMovie()
```

Both require that the component already be in your Library. This is something of a bummer because it means that components can't really be added dynamically. That is, you can't create one out of thin air with your code. The component *must* already be in your Library.

Adding a Component to the Library

The easiest way to add a component to the Library is to drag the component you want to use—for example, a Button or a CheckBox—to the Stage, then delete it. This adds the component to your Library. And no, you can't drag it directly to the Library—it won't work that way (be cool if it did, though).

You can also (this is the harder way, with no huge gain) add a keyframe that the timeline never gets to, and add the components to that keyframe. For example, if your entire movie takes place on one frame, add a `stop()` to that frame. Then, in frame 2, put all of the form components.

For an example of the preferred (by me) drag-and-delete way, open a new file, drag a Button and a CheckBox onto the Stage, and then delete them. Your Library should look like the screenshot in Figure 5.2.

Adding a Component Using attachMovie()

Now that the component is in your Library, you can actually do something with it. If you haven't used `attachMovie()` before, it's pretty simple. All it does is piggyback a movie onto another one (more detail in Topic 19, Attaching Movies).

Put this code on the first frame:

Figure 5.2
And Lo, They Were Placed into Yon Library— And It Was Good

```
this.attachMovie("Button", "button1", 1, {label: "Click me now,
    darn it!"});
```

Test the movie, and you get the button shown in Figure 5.3.

Good news: The button appeared. Bad news: It's too small. We'll fix that in a sec.

Click me now, da

Figure 5.3
Click Me Now Button—But Too Small

What Happened

- First, by using `this`, we make it clear that the main movie (the one the button attaches to) is the main movie, the root timeline, the Big Kahuna of the Stage.

- Next, we say that we're creating an instance of `"Button"` and calling that instance `"button1"`.

- We're placing that instance on level 1.

- The thing with the curly braces is an object property, which puts actual words on the button. It's exactly like saying

  ```
  button1.label = "Click me now, darn it!";
  ```

In Case You Forgot

When you added the Button component to the Library, it gets the identifier *Button*, which you use in `attachMovie()`. Right-click (Mac: control-click) the

Figure 5.4

*Linkage
Properties Box*

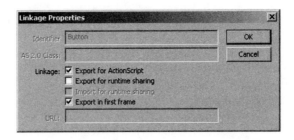

Button in the Library and choose Linkage..., and you get the Linkage Properties box shown in Figure 5.4.

See the grayed-out identifier Button?

How to Fix the Size

We need to make the button wider (default width is 100 pixels, default height, 22 pixels). Since you've used movie clips before, you're probably used to changing `_width` and `_height` to size it, right? That won't work for components—it just stretches them out.

Try this:

```
button1.setSize(150, 22);
```

Test the movie, and you get the button shown in Figure 5.5.

Yup. Darn straight.

Adding a Component Using createClassObject()

At this point in its life, the new `createClassObject()` method is almost identical to `attachMovie()`.

First of all, if you have no real idea what a class is, you should check out Topic 41, Your First Class, right now. Are you going? You should go. . . . I don't hear pages flipping!

Now that you understand what a class is, here's how to add a checkbox:

```
this.createClassObject(mx.controls.CheckBox, "cb", 1, {label:"Check
   this"});
```

The only real difference from `attachMovie()` is that instead of using the symbol's ID, we use the class name.

You can see the `CheckBox` class yourself. Find the Flash MX 2004 folder, navigate down `en/FirstRun/Classes/mx/controls`, and you'll find `CheckBox.as`. Check it out (but don't change it unless you know exactly what you're doing).

Figure 5.5

*Click Me Now
Button—Just
the Right Size*

Click me now, darn it!

How to Choose?

The ActionScript manual wants us to use **createClassObject()**, but it is a little unclear on why. I don't think it matters at all which one you use. The only possible advantage I can see to using **createClassObject()** is that the method is probably bound for greater functionality in future versions of Flash, and it may help if you get used to it now so you can take advantage of it later.

But that's pretty thin reasoning. Either method is fine to use.

The move() method comes from the UIObject class, not from UIComponent. It's easy to forget and use moveTo(), but that won't work here. moveTo() is just for movie clips.

```
component.move(x,y)
movieClip.moveTo(x,y)
```

Here's another way to think of attachMovie() and createClassObject():

attachMovie() brings out the symbol. The symbol then finds the class.
createClassObject() finds the class first, then brings out the associated symbol.

That is all.

6

Creating a Form from Scratch

 ometimes, you want to create a form from scratch, which means

- Creating all the text fields using ActionScript instead of creating them during authoring.
- No TextInput or TextArea components.

No, really—it could happen. Whenever I say I'll never need to use something, it guarantees that within the week, I'll be using it.

The only reasons you would want to create a form from scratch are these:

- Regular text fields take much less memory than TextInput and TextArea components, resulting in a smaller file size.
- You just like working with text fields. You're like that.

We're going to create a form with nine text fields. Creating them from scratch results in a 2K SWF file. If we used TextInput components to create the same form, it would be 27K. So, if you're sensitive to download times, you might want to stick with text fields.

DO OR DIE:

> > You can use createTextField() instead of TextInput and TextArea components.

> > Using createTextField() can result in a much smaller file size.

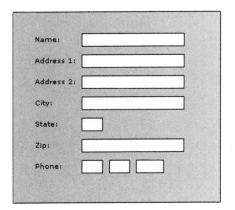

Notice I'm not talking about creating radio buttons or checkboxes from scratch. You can do it, of course, but honestly, it's something of a pain, and I'd need a darn good reason to do it. So, it makes sense to learn about text fields.

Figure 6.1

Form Without a Background

It will help some if you download this movie from www.wire-man.com/garage. The unfinished and finished versions are there.

Let's make a simple form that gathers basic address information. Nothing too fancy, but darn common.

It ends up looking like the screenshot in Figure 6.1—rather boring without the background, isn't it.

Enough! Code fix!

```
var form:MovieClip = this.createEmptyMovieClip("form", 1);
form._x = 30;
```

The reason this **form** movie clip exists is because we're going to put all of our text fields in it, and dumping them in a single container makes them easy to move around the Stage. You always want to handle one movie clip instead of, say, nine.

In addition to a little variable textFieldHeight (which is in the movie), we create the movie clip that holds all of our text fields.

```
var form:MovieClip = this.createEmptyMovieClip("form", 1);
```

We could also code

```
this.createEmptyMovieClip("form", 1);
```

for the same result. I like adding the var part because it makes the code easier to read. I immediately know there's a movie clip called "form" without having to wade through the whole createEmptyMovieClip() thing. I'm a busy guy.

Next, we create all the labels (not component Labels, just text fields that act as labels).

```
var textFieldHeight:Number = 18;

with (form) {
    createTextField("name_label", 1, 0, 30, 150, textFieldHeight);
    name_label.text = "Name: ";
    createTextField("address1_label", 2, 0, 60, 150,
      textFieldHeight);
    address1_label.text = "Address 1: ";
    createTextField("address2_label", 3, 0, 90, 150,
      textFieldHeight);
    address2_label.text = "Address 2: ";
    createTextField("city_label", 4, 0, 120, 150, textFieldHeight);
    city_label.text = "City: ";
    createTextField("state_label", 5, 0, 150, 150,
      textFieldHeight);
    state_label.text = "State: ";
    createTextField("zip_label", 6, 0, 180, 150, textFieldHeight);
    zip_label.text = "Zip: ";
    createTextField("phone_label", 7, 0, 210, 150,
      textFieldHeight);
    phone_label.text = "Phone: ";
}
```

Test the movie. It should look something like the screenshot in Figure 6.2.

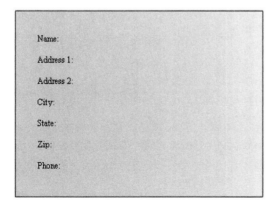

Figure 6.2

*Form Without
Input Text Fields*

Now, let's add the input text fields. Put the following after the `phone_label` line and before the }.

```
createTextField("name_txt", 10, fieldEdgeX, 30, 150,
  textFieldHeight);
name_txt.border = true;
name_txt.type = "input";
name_txt.background = true;
name_txt.backgroundColor = "0xFFFFFF";

createTextField("address1_txt", 11, fieldEdgeX, 60, 150,
  textFieldHeight);
address1_txt.border = true;
address1_txt.type = "input";
address1_txt.background = true;
address1_txt.backgroundColor = "0xFFFFFF";

createTextField("address2_txt", 12, fieldEdgeX, 90, 150,
  textFieldHeight);
address2_txt.border = true;
address2_txt.type = "input";
address2_txt.background = true;
address2_txt.backgroundColor = "0xFFFFFF";

createTextField("city_txt", 13, fieldEdgeX, 120, 150,
  textFieldHeight);
city_txt.border = true;
city_txt.type = "input";
city_txt.background = true;
city_txt.backgroundColor = "0xFFFFFF";

createTextField("state_txt", 14, fieldEdgeX, 150, 30,
  textFieldHeight);
state_txt.border = true;
state_txt.type = "input";
state_txt.maxChars = 2;
state_txt.restrict = "A-Z";
state_txt.background = true;
state_txt.backgroundColor = "0xFFFFFF";

createTextField("zip_txt", 15, fieldEdgeX, 180, 150, textFieldHeight);
zip_txt.border = true;
zip_txt.type = "input";
zip_txt.maxChars = 5;
```

```
zip_txt.restrict = "0-9";
zip_txt.background = true;
zip_txt.backgroundColor = "0xFFFFFF";

createTextField("phoneAreaCode_txt", 16, fieldEdgeX, 210, 30,
  textFieldHeight);
phoneAreaCode_txt.border = true;
phoneAreaCode_txt.type = "input";
phoneAreaCode_txt.maxChars = 3;
phoneAreaCode_txt.restrict = "0-9";
phoneAreaCode_txt.background = true;
phoneAreaCode_txt.backgroundColor = "0xFFFFFF";

createTextField("phonePrefix_txt", 17, fieldEdgeX + 40, 210, 30,
  textFieldHeight);
phonePrefix_txt.border = true;
phonePrefix_txt.type = "input";
phonePrefix_txt.maxChars = 3;
phonePrefix_txt.restrict = "0-9";
phonePrefix_txt.background = true;
phonePrefix_txt.backgroundColor = "0xFFFFFF";

createTextField("phoneSuffix_txt", 18, fieldEdgeX + 80, 210, 40,
  textFieldHeight);
phoneSuffix_txt.border = true;
phoneSuffix_txt.type = "input";
phoneSuffix_txt.maxChars = 4;
phoneSuffix_txt.restrict = "0-9";
phoneSuffix_txt.background = true;
phoneSuffix_txt.backgroundColor = "0xFFFFFF";
```

Test your movie. It should resemble Figure 6.3.

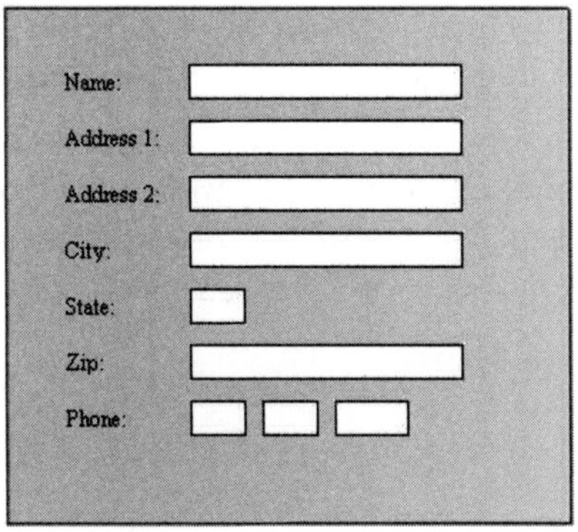

Figure 6.3

*A Form Ready
for Input*

What We Did

We used

```
with(form) { ... }
```

instead of writing out

```
form.createTextField("name_txt", 10, fieldEdgeX, 30, 150,
  textFieldHeight);
form.name_txt.border = true;
form.name_txt.type = "input";
form.name_txt.background = true;
form.name_txt.backgroundColor = "0xFFFFFF";
```

over and over again. It's just a typing shortcut.

```
createTextField ("fieldName", depth, x, y, width, height)
```

It's pretty self-explanatory. Notice all our fields are at different depths (also known as levels). Only one movie clip, text field, or thing can be on a level at once, so if you have something on level 1, then try to place something else there, the new thing will replace the old thing.

```
fieldEdgeX
```

This variable just made it easier to align all of the text fields at once.

```
textFieldHeight
```

Same story as for adding the input text fields—it's just easier to set all the text fields with the same value. Also, we get to experiment to see what height works best without having to change every single text field individually.

```
textField.restrict = "A-Z";
textField.restrict = "0-9";
```

This is a simplified form of regular expressions. In the top line, we tell Flash that only letters (uppercase and lowercase are fine) are allowed. In the bottom line, we say that only numbers can go there. If the user tries to type anything else, nothing appears in the text field.

By the way, when you create text fields via ActionScript, they're automatically dynamic text fields (as opposed to static or input) unless you specify otherwise. The rest you can figure out yourself (you know what a border is).

<geek aside>

All over slashdot today about Dungeons & Dragons turning 30. I spent much of my wildly awkward junior high years playing D&D, and I don't regret a minute of it (I was so dorky my little sister once beat someone up who insisted that she and I were related). I also played in college some, which may explain why it took five full years to graduate. Those guys I played with now play fantasy baseball. You ask me, it's the same darn game.

</geek aside>

7

Validating Form Data

One of the easiest ways to keep track of your form elements is to put all of your form components and such into an empty movie clip container called **form**. Try it; it's easy. It'll help you keep everything together in a nice, neat package, and that usually pays off in the computer world.

I'm assuming you already know how to use these components (or can learn very fast). That is, you can populate a ComboBox by creating an array and using **dataProvider**. Did that make any sense? If not, well, read the code carefully. You're a sport—you can keep up.

DO OR DIE:

> > This topic is about how to access form data. For example, how do you see the number of list items chosen, what date the user likes, or which checkbox or radio button is chosen?

> > Parsing the content of text fields also happens here—that is, parsing strings to find phone numbers, email addresses, and so on.

ComboBoxes

Create an empty movie clip called **form**. Drag a ComboBox component into it and call it **states_cbx**. Go back to the main scene and drag the form clip onto it.

If you use an array as a **dataProvider**, you'll want an array of objects, like this:

```
// Create Array
states_array = new Array();
states_array.push({data:"", label:"Choose a state"});
```

```
states_array.push({data:"AL", label:"Alabama"});
states_array.push({data:"AK", label:"Alaska"});
states_array.push({data:"AZ", label:"Arizona"});
states_array.push({data:"AR", label:"Arkansas"});
states_array.push({data:"CA", label:"California"});
```

Then, assuming your ComboBox is called `states_cbx`,

```
form.states_cbx.dataProvider = states_array;
// "Choose a state" is longer than default component size
form.states_cbx.setSize(150);
```

test the movie, and you get a ComboBox like the one in Figure 7.1.

Reading from a ComboBox

Reading from a ComboBox looks something like this:

```
form.validate_btn.onRelease = function()
{
    // find out what the user chose on the states combo box
    if (form.states_cbx.selectedItem.data != "")
    {
            trace("User chose: " + form.states_cbx.selectedItem.label);
    }
    else
    {
            Alert.show("show me a darn alert!");
    }
}
```

The thing you care about here is `selectedItem`. That's the chunk of code that finds which item the user chose from the drop-down menu (I use drop-down menu interchangeably with ComboBox because drop-down makes a heck of a lot more sense to me than ComboBox, which sounds like something you'd buy at Burger King).

You can also use `selectedIndex`. This returns the index of the selected item. The first item is 0, the second is 1, and so on.

Figure 7.1
*A Little
ComboBox*

```
/* using selectedIndex */
form.validate_btn.onRelease = function()
{
    if (form.states_cbx.selectedIndex != 0)
    {
```

```
        s = form.states_cbx.selectedIndex;
        // the following doesn't work
        trace("User chose: " + form.states_cbx[s].label);

        // you have to use the getItemAt() method
        trace("User really chose: " +
                form.states_cbx.getItemAt(s).label);
    }
    else
    {
        alert.show("show me a darn alert!");
    }
}
```

Reading an Editable ComboBox

You can make a ComboBox editable with the following line:

```
form.states_cbx.editable = true;
```

This clears out the combo text field, as in Figure 7.2.

The user can now type in it, as in Figure 7.3.

How do you get that value? `selectedItem` or `selectedIndex` won't do you any good—as soon as you say your ComboBox is editable, those properties immediately become "undefined" (and don't change unless the user reselects something from the drop-down menu). To get to this user-entered value, you have to use this code:

```
form.validate_btn.onRelease = function()
{
    trace(form.states_cbx.value);
}
```

That's the only way to get the value from an edited field in a ComboBox. The value property can also be useful in a non-editable ComboBox (called

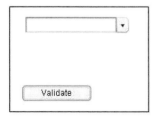

Figure 7.2

Cleared-Out Editable Text Field

Figure 7.3

Editing the ComboBox's Text Field

static ComboBoxes). In this example, if the user chooses Alaska, then the value property equals Alaska.

> **DOC ALERT.**
> The documentation says that value looks at data first, then at label. Wrong. It looks at label first.

Checkbox

This is really simple. We just want to know if a checkbox has been checked or not.

```
form.spam_chk.label = "Please send me spam, I mean product updates.";
form.spam_chk.setSize(300);

form.validate_btn.onRelease = function()
{
    if (form.spam_chk.selected)
    {
        trace("spam spam spam spam spam !");
    }
}
```

Ta-da!

Radio Buttons

Start with three radio button components dragged to the Stage. Call them red_radio, green_radio, and blue_radio. Put this code in the beginning, not inside the button event handler (that's the **onRelease** function).

```
// Set radio buttons
red_radio.groupName = "tintGroup";
green_radio.groupName = "tintGroup";
blue_radio.groupName = "tintGroup";

red_radio.data = "red";
red_radio.label = "Red";
green_radio.data = "green";
green_radio.label = "Green";
```

```
blue_radio.data = "blue";
blue_radio.label = "Blue";
```

Here's the code (this is inside the `onRelease` function).

```
if (form.tintGroup.getValue())
{
    trace("they choose a color: " + form.tintGroup.getValue());
}
else
{

    trace("no color");
    // little bonus undocumented method here:
    // you can disable a whole group of radio buttons at one go
    form.tintGroup.setEnabled(false);
}
```

The Flash documentation is a little thin when it comes to discovering which radio button was chosen. It says, like, nothing. But as it turns out, `getValue()` returns the data portion of the selected radio button.

This method comes from the `RadioButtonGroup` class (line 110 in `RadioButtonGroup.as`, if you're super-interested). I kinda wish it was documented.

Reading a DataGrid

According to Macromedia's online manual (http://www.macromedia.com/livedocs/), the `DataGrid` component allows you to create powerful data-enabled displays and applications.

It's useful to think of a `DataGrid` as a table, with rows and columns.

`DataGrid`, as it turns out, is very special, and we can't just look at it like any other component. We have to attach a listener to it and see when someone clicks on a cell (more on listeners in Topic 45, `on()` and `onClipEvent()`).

Setting up variables is done like this:

```
// track if grid row's been selected
var gridSelected:Boolean;
var selectedGridRow:Number;
```

Then, out of laziness, we do this:

```
// Set data grid
states_grid.dataProvider = states_array;
states_grid.setSize(300,100);
```

Finally, we write the *outside*-of-the-button validation function:

```
// datagrid needs different treatment
var gridListener = new Object();
gridListener.cellPress = function (evt)
{
    gridSelected = true;
    selectedGridRow =
        form.states_grid.getItemAt(evt.itemIndex).label;
}
form.states_grid.addEventListener("cellPress", gridListener);
```

Holy Chainsaw Massacre! What the heck is this?

This is a listener and an event handler, which we haven't covered yet. There's more information in Topic 45, but for a quick explanation, here goes:

Events are things that happen in the Flash movie, like the user pressing a button, the mouse moving, or an XML file finishing loading. A chunk of code that's fired off when an event happens is called an *event handler*. In earlier versions of Flash, this looked like on(release), onClipEvent(enterFrame), and so on. The onRelease function above is an event handler.

Sometimes, ActionScript requires that you get a little fancier than just using an event handler. You have to create an object whose only purpose in life is to wait for a specific event to happen (that's gridListener here). When that listener sees the event occur, it rushes off to the appropriate event handler, in this case gridListener.cellPress.

When an event happens, all the information about the event—what it was, what object it happened to, where on the Stage it occurred—is passed to the event handler. That's what evt is—the event object that has all that information. In this case, the event happened to a DataGrid, so there's a little itemIndex property in the event object.

Finally, in the validation function, we have the following:

```
// validate data grid
// that is, make sure something is selected
if (gridSelected)
{
    trace("grid: " + selectedGridRow);
}
else
{
    trace("You no select grid! You crazy?!");
}
```

And that's it for DataGrid.

TextInput, TextArea, and Regular Input Text Fields

There are several ways to check if something's been entered in a `TextInput` or `TextArea` component, or in a text field. One is to see if the length of the entered text is zero (or undefined).

Is anything entered?

```
// make sure something is entered in the textInput component
if (!form.myText_txt.length)
{
    trace("type something in textInput thingie.");
}
/*  You can also use
    if (!form.myText_txt.text) and
    if (form.myText_txt.length == 0) and
    if (form.myText_txt.text == "")

    You can't use
    if (form.myText_txt.text == undefined)
    if (form.myText_txt.length == undefined)
*/
```

In the uncommented code, we say, "If there's no length, then. . . ." Dialing up the geek, we test if the `length` property evaluates to true or false. Because it's equal to zero, it evaluates to false, which leaves us with

```
if (!false)
```

which results in

```
if (true)
```

As you can see from the commented code, you can do the same thing with the **text** property. Length just looks at how many characters are in the text field, while **text** knows exactly what those characters are.

Why can't you use "undefined"? It's the obvious answer: because they aren't undefined. Length equals zero and **text** equals "", which are both different than undefined.

Is the Right Thing Entered?

Sadly, there are no real, regular expressions in ActionScript. You can use the **restrict** property, but for real data-cleaning, you need to use a server-side script.

A common example in computer books is to see whether or not the user entered a real email address. The thing is, it's trivial to enter a bogus email address, so I think the only reason to check for a real email address format is if you require an email for account verification or something (that is, the user signs up for something). You send the user an email with an account activation link—to make sure the email address is real—which he or she clicks, and lo! The user has an account.

Okay, so there's one reason to check for an email address, and it's simple enough. Let's try it. We'll use `email_txt`, which is a plain ol' text field, not a component or anything.

```
// email validation for email_txt
atIndex = form.email_txt.text.indexOf("@");
dotIndex = form.email_txt.text.lastIndexOf(".");
if (atIndex<0 || dotIndex<2 || atIndex>=dotIndex)
{
    trace("Please enter a valid email address.");
}
```

This also works if the user doesn't enter anything in the email field. Notice the `lastIndexOf()`. You've gotta use that, or else

```
a.s@s.com
```

causes an error (because the first "." occurs before the "@").

The whole

```
form.email_txt.text.indexOf("@")
```

may be a little intimidating, but worry not. Separate it out:

```
Say form.email_txt.text is "a.s@s.com"
```

which evaluates to

```
"a.s@s.com".indexOf("@")
```

Okay, this isn't proper syntax, but we're just looking at the idea here.

Note that `form.email_txt.indexOf()` won't work. `indexOf()` has to be connected to a string. Thus,

```
form.email_txt.text.indexOf("@")
```

Alert

The alert component is a little window that looks something like Figure 7.4.

Possible buttons that can appear on an Alert window thingie include

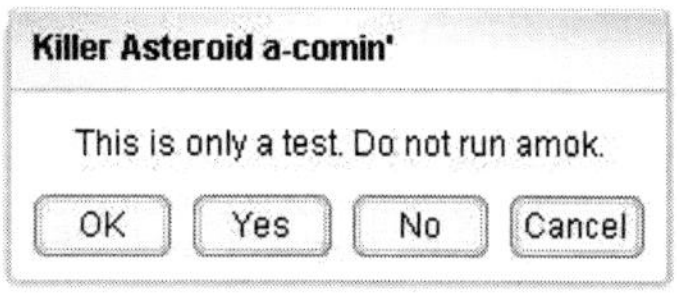

- OK
- No
- Yes
- Cancel

Figure 7.4

*The Alert
Component*

The only thing you can do with the Alert is tell which of four possible buttons was pressed (and any one of the four, all four, or any combination may be visible).

This component has a call to an event handler built into its syntax, so go ahead and use it.

```
alertHandler = function(evt){
    trace (evt.detail + "was clicked");
    /*
            Yes:        evt.detail = 1
            No:         evt.detail = 2
            OK:         evt.detail = 4
            Cancel:     evt.detail = 8
    */
}


// displays buttons in this order no matter what:
// OK, Yes, No, Cancel
Alert.show("This is only a test. Do not run amok.", "Killer
Asteroid a-comin'", Alert.YES | Alert.NO | Alert.OK | Alert.CANCEL,
this, alertHandler);
```

List

Like the ComboBox, List uses an array of objects with data and label properties.

Let's start over for this one—the other form was getting too crowded.

```
#include "statesArray.as"

// remove the first item, since that's the "Choose.." one
states_array.shift();
states_list.dataProvider = states_array;
states_list.setSize(200, 150);
```

```
validate_btn.onRelease = function()
{
    statesChosen = states_list.selectedItems;
    numStatesChosen = statesChosen.length;
    if (numStatesChosen > 0)
    {
        for (i=0; i<statesChosen.length; i++)
        {
            trace(statesChosen[i].data);
        }
    }
    else
    {
        trace("choose a state!");
    }
}
```

DateField

You can figure this one out from the code. I'm exhausted.

```
// Is there a date?
userDate = form.start_date.selectedDate
if (userDate)
{
    // make sure date is within a certain range
    var maxYear:Number = 2007;
    if (userDate.getYear() > maxYear)
    {
        trace("your date is too future-y.")
    }
} else {
    trace("bad date");
}
```

Submitting a Form and Getting Data Back

DO OR DIE:

> > LoadVars

> > LoadVars.send()

> > LoadVars.sendAndLoad()

his topic is all about the LoadVars objects, because that's the best way to deal with form-based data (or any data that's not XML). To submit a form, you cram all your data into a LoadVars object before sending it off to some server somewhere, and it's into a LoadVars object that incoming data from servers is crammed.

Cram. Heh. When it comes to name/value pair data (as opposed to XML), LoadVars is your buddy and pal. LoadVars would never hit on your girlfriend, no matter how drunk it got. Well, it might flirt a little, but *that's it*.

LoadVars is a nice way to package variables to send to a server—you get to decide exactly what goes and what doesn't, so you can manipulate variables before sending them off into the ether.

Here's how we do it. First, create some form with a text field (name_txt) and a submit button. The code on the first frame goes like this:

```
submit_btn.onRelease = function() {
    var formData:Object = new LoadVars();
}
```

Next, we add the text fields (non-component ones), **TextInputs**, and **TextArea**, which is darn simple.

```
/*****
*    Form submission
******/
toWireMan = new LoadVars();
fromWireMan = new LoadVars();

// When user clicks in the text field, the
// text already there disappears
name_txt.onSetFocus = function () {
    this.text = "";
}

submit_btn.onPress = function ()
{
    toWireMan.name = _root.name_txt.text;
    _root.name_txt.text = "loading...";
    toWireMan.sendAndLoad("receiveData.php3", fromWireMan);
}

fromWireMan.onLoad = function () {
    _root.name_txt.text = this.newName;
}
```

What the Sam Hill?

We have a few new things here. Clear your head. Get a glass of water if you need one. I'm throwing a couple things at you at once.

First, we create a couple of **LoadVars** objects, but we don't do anything with them.

```
toWireMan = new LoadVars();
fromWireMan = new LoadVars();
```

Then, we wait until a user clicks the submit button.

```
submit_btn.onPress = function ()
{
    ...
}
```

We then add a variable to one of the `LoadVars` objects.

```
toWireMan.name = _root.name_txt.text;
```

We let the user know that something's going on.

```
_root.name_txt.text = "loading...";
```

Then we do the heavy lifting.

```
toWireMan.sendAndLoad("receiveData.php3", fromWireMan);
```

This takes the data in the `toWireMan` object (just the name at this point), and sends it to `receive.php3`, which presumably does something that processes this information. Any information that comes back from `receiveData.php3` is placed into the `fromWireMan` object.

Our little PHP page is just this:

```
<?
    if ($name == "Dan") {
        echo "newName=Annie";
    } else {
        echo "newName=Poopdeck";
    }
?>
```

You can figure out the advanced logic utilized here. The `$name` is indeed the very same name that's in `toWireMan`. Notice that the PHP never sees anything called `toWireMan`—it sees only the data inside.

This data is sent via `POST`, if you were wondering. (As you might guess, there's also a method called just `send()`. Use `send()` when you not only want to send data to a page, but also want the browser to go to that page.)

Let's see how to deal with data using other form elements.

Checkboxes

Add a checkbox component and call it `spam_chk`. In the `onRelease` event handler, add the following:

```
// find and load the selected checkboxes
toWireMan.spam = (spam_chk.selected) ? true : false;
```

If you haven't seen this way of doing an if statement, it's pretty cool.

```
var = (condition) ? value if true : value if false;
```

Radio Buttons

If you're pulling information from a group of radio buttons, use this:

```
toWireMan.madScientist = madScientists.selectedData;
```

That `selectedData` thing is pretty handy. Make sure you've actually set the data property of the buttons, either via ActionScript or by direct authoring.

List

List is similar to ComboBox:

```
#include "statesArray.as" // this is on my web site
states_array.shift();
states_list.dataProvider = states_array;
states_list.setSize(150,100);
```

Then, in the `onRelease` handler,

```
// parse out data from list
var stateData_array:Array = new Array();
for (i=0; i<states_list.selectedItems.length; i++)
{
    stateData_array.push(states_list.selectedItems[i].data);
}
// results in states=AL,AK,AZ,AR (or whatever states the user
// selected)
toWireMan.states = stateData_array;
```

If you just do

```
toWireMan.states = states_list.selectedItems;
```

you get

```
states=[object Object],[object Object],[object Object]
```

which helps no one.

The same code works for DataGrid (and just use `.data` for ComboBox).

DateField

The Datefield component just passes a string. Have to use the **Date** object to pull anything useful out of it.

```
// pull out date
var userDate:Date = start_date.selectedDate;
toWireMan.date = (userDate.getMonth()+1) + "/" +
    userDate.getDate() + "/" +
    userDate.getFullYear();
```

Here's the whole thing:

```
/*****
*    Form submission
******/
#include "statesArray.as"

toWireMan = new LoadVars();
fromWireMan = new LoadVars();

states_array.shift();
states_list.dataProvider = states_array;
states_list.setSize(150,100);

name_txt.onSetFocus = function ()
{
    this.text = "";
}

submit_btn.onPress = function ()
{
    // load up the LoadVars object
    toWireMan.name = _root.name_txt.text;

    // find and load the selected checkboxes
    toWireMan.spam  = (spam_chk.selected) ? true : false;

    // find out which mad scientist was chosen
    toWireMan.madScientist = madScientists.selectedData;
```

```
        // parse out data from list
        var stateData_array:Array = new Array();
        for (i=0; i<states_list.selectedItems.length; i++)
        {
                stateData_array.push(states_list.selectedItems[i].data);
        }
        // results in states=AL,AK,AZ,AR
        // (or whatever states the user selected)
        toWireMan.states = stateData_array;

        /*
                if you just do
                toWireMan.states = states_list.selectedItems;
                you get
                states=[object Object],[object Object],[object Object]
        */

        // pull out date
        var userDate:Date = start_date.selectedDate;
        toWireMan.date = (userDate.getMonth()+1) + "/" +
                userDate.getDate() + "/" + userDate.getFullYear();



        // fire off data to server
        _root.name_txt.text = "loading...";
        toWireMan.send("receiveData.php3", "_self");
        //toWireMan.sendAndLoad("receiveData.php3", fromWireMan);
}

fromWireMan.onLoad = function ()
{
    _root.name_txt.text = this.newName + this.spam;
    mad_txt.text = this.mad;
}
```

The PHP for displaying results follows (sorry, my lame ISP only supports PHP3):

```
<? //echo $name;

    if ($name == "Dan") {
            echo "newName=Annie";
```

```php
} else {
        echo "newName=Poopdeck";
}
echo "&";
if ($spam == "true") {
        echo "spam=pr0n";
} else {
        echo "spam=mortgage";
}
echo "&";
echo "mad=$madScientist";

echo "states=$states";
echo "<br><br>";
echo "date = $date";
?>
```

Form Screens

Screens and slides are new in MX2004. With these features, it's like having a PowerPoint functionality built into Flash. That is, you can create a bunch of slides with movie clips, form elements, and so on.

We don't cover the little details of how to create screens and slides here. We do a quick overview and then dive into some code. Personally, I'm not a huge fan of form screens, but perhaps I just need to get used to them. I like the idea, but I'm not sure I like the thing. Kind of like jazz. And plays. And tea.

Overview

A Screen file is different than a regular Flash movie. It's something you choose when you first create a file, as shown in Figure 9.1.

You then create a couple of screens, put some elements on them, and get a result similar to Figure 9.2.

Typically, the main screen ("application" in this case) is empty—it's more of a container for all the other screens.

Figure 9.1

*And Lo, a Screen
Was Chosen*

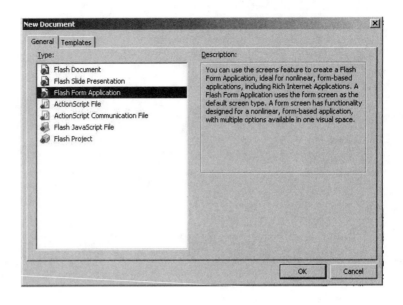

A Cool Thing

A cool thing about the screens (as opposed to the slides) is that the user's movement through the screens doesn't have to be linear—you can toss in logic that diverts a user from one set of screens to another. This could be handy, because you can present different screens based on what the user does.

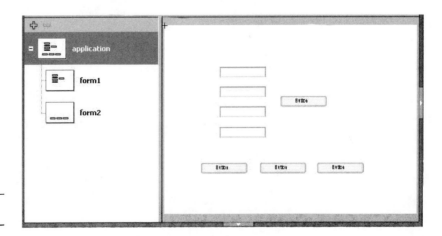

Figure 9.2

*Very Simple
Screen File*

Code Fix!

Since we don't want both forms (that's **form1** and **form2**) to be visible at the same time, let's hide the second one.

```
_root.application.form2.visible = false;
```

The only other thing we care about here is moving from one form to the next: when the user clicks a Next button, the old form should disappear and the new one should become visible. Let's write a function that takes care of that.

```
function nextScreen(oldFormName, nextFormName)
{
    this[oldFormName].visible = false;
    this[nextFormName].visible = true;
}
```

Not too tough, eh? Remember that this is in the application screen, so **this** refers to **application**. We could also write this as

```
function nextScreen(oldFormName, nextFormName)
{
    _root.application[oldFormName].visible = false;
    _root.application[nextFormName].visible = true;
}
```

Since **application** is a container for all the other screens, the other screens act as children to **application**.

Now, in the **form1** screen, there's a button called **form1_btn**. Here's some code on **form1**'s first frame:

```
form1_btn.onRelease = function ()
{
    _parent.nextScreen("form1", "form2");
}
```

Since **form1** is a child of **application**, we use **_parent** to find **application** and see the **nextScreen** function there. We could have used the following as well:

```
form1_btn.onRelease = function ()
{
    _root.application.nextScreen("form1", "form2");
}
```

There's also a property called rootScreen, which is a direct reference to the top-level screen (again, application).

```
form1_btn.onRelease = function ()
{
    rootScreen.nextScreen("form1", "form2");
}
```

It works the same as the others.
By the way,

```
this.rootScreen.nextScreen("form1", "form2");
```

doesn't work. Leave off the this.

FAQ

Tom Asks Why

Why bother with forms or screens? Honestly, I haven't found much of a need for them in my work, but it's possible I'm just not used to them yet. The screens can be useful for a wizard in which a user must move through several discrete screens.

Extras

There isn't much more to talk about regarding screens except for the on(reveal) method, timelines, and event listeners.

on(reveal)

When a screen appears, it's a reveal event, so if you want some code to run when a screen becomes visible, use the following:

```
on(reveal)
{
    // code
}
```

Screens and Timelines

Screens are descendents of MoveClip, and they do have timelines even if they're hidden from view. You can create animations on them and do everything you might want to do on a normal movie clip.

However, the whole point of using screens is to avoid the timeline. So, if you decide you need a timeline, you may want to ask yourself whether you should even be using form screens instead of regular ol' movie clips and frames.

Screens and Event Listeners

Note that all the events for screens (and slides, which we are loathe to sully our hands with) are exposed using the event listener system. This means you have to use listener objects to get functions to run when certain events happen. That is, this code will work:

```
loadListener = new Object();
loadListener.load = function {
    // do stuff. Impress me!
}
this.addEventListener("load", loadListener);
```

this refers to the screen itself.

The following code won't work:

```
this.onLoad = function() {
    // do stuff
}
```

Screen inherits from the Loader component (which makes sense), while each screen is an instance of the mx.screens.Form class. A screen can also be a class—click on a screen and look at its properties (see Figure 9.3).

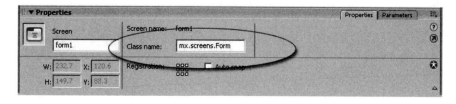

Figure 9.3
A Screen's Class

PART II

Skinning Components

10

Setting Skins and Styles: Halo and Sample

et's start at the beginning here: when you're dealing with components and you want to change their appearance, you have two choices:

- Setting styles
- Skinning

All components are made up of a lot of little movie clips that are pulled together by Flash. Behind all of these components there's also a ton of ActionScript that pulls together the movie clips and gives them behaviors, but this code is hidden from you, so we won't spend time talking about that here.

Those little movie clips are called skins. When we talk about a component's skin, we mean all of the movie clips and graphics that make up an entire component. Thus, if you "skin" a component, you change those little movie clips into what you want them to be.

When we use styles to change the appearance of a component, we use ActionScript to change the color of some of the component's movie clips (or skins). There is a limited number (a couple dozen) of styles that you can change about a component: text color, shadow color, border color, and so on.

Skinning a component (changing its little movie clips directly) gives you much more control over it, while using styles is simpler and easier but gives you much less control.

Got it? Ready for the next thing? Good.

Themes are collections of skins and styles. For example, the collection of component skins that Flash automatically loads with is called Halo. Another theme called Sample is also available.

Halo components have a certain look, and Sample components have a slightly different, more angular look. This is because Halo skins have rounded corners, and Sample skins have sharp corners. See Figure 10.1 and Figure 10.2.

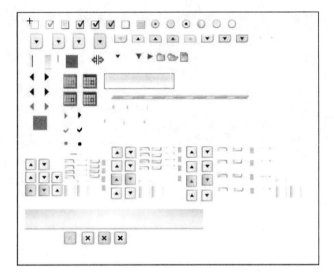

Figure 10.1

All the Halo Skins

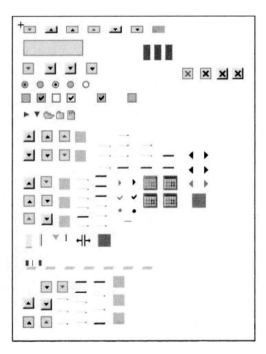

Figure 10.2

All the Sample Skins

The Sample theme allows you to experiment with the full set of styles available to version 2 components. The Halo theme uses only a subset of the available styles. I don't know why.

Dealing with Halo's themeColors

As a theme, Halo has a feature that other themes don't: `themeColor`. If you've used the default components, you've noticed that they use a number of shades of green when you roll over or click them. Halo has a property that sets those colors—it's called `themeColor`, and its default value is `haloGreen`.

To set all your component to `haloGreen`, use the following code:

```
_global.style.setStyle("themeColor", "haloGreen");
```

What kinds of Halo are available besides `haloGreen`?

- `haloBlue`
- `haloOrange`

You can choose any color, though:

```
componentInstanceName.setStyle("themeColor", 0xFF0000); // red
_global.style.setStyle("themeColor", 0x9AC54F); // baby puke
```

All of the following work:

```
_global.style.setStyle("themeColor", "haloGreen");
_global.style.setStyle("themeColor", 0xFF0000);
button1_btn.setStyle("themeColor", "haloBlue");
button1_btn.setStyle("themeColor", 0x0000FF);
```

The movie clips that set what Halo and Sample look like are

- `Flash MX 2004/en/FirstRun/ComponentFLA/HaloTheme.fla`
- `Flash MX 2004/en/FirstRun/ComponentFLA/SampleTheme.fla`

Go ahead—open them up, poke through them. You'll get a better idea of what a theme is once you see them and run through all the folders in their libraries.

Switching from Halo to Sample

Since the Halo theme is the default theme, if you want your components to use any other theme, you have to explicitly tell Flash to use another set of component skins. Here's how you do it:

1. Open your movie file.
2. Open up `SampleTheme.fla`. You'll find it in the main `Flash MX Professional 2004 folder/en/FirstRun/ComponentFLA/SampleTheme.fla`.
3. Open the Library of `SampleTheme.fla`.
4. Switch to your movie.
5. Drag the Flash UI Components 2 folder to your movie's Stage and delete it. This adds those component parts to your movie.
6. Add components to your movie and test it! The new components from `SampleTheme.fla` are there, with their nice sharp edges.

11

Setting Styles on a Single Component

All you can do using ActionScript alone is change the color of certain component parts: text, background color, border, and so on. Only some of these parts can be changed using ActionScript, so if you want to really muck with the appearance of a component, you have to skin it, which is discussed in Topic 14, Skinning Components. It's definitely more involved than setting styles. So, if you want to alter the appearance of a component, try setting styles through ActionScript first. If that doesn't work, move on to skinning.

Changing a single component is pretty simple, if somewhat limited as far as usefulness goes. Here's the syntax.

```
myComponent.setStyle("thingToChange", colorOrStyle);
```

Table 11.1 lists the styles you can use. Note that some of them require that you use the Sample theme—some of them have no effect in Halo.

Some styles are rectangle-specific:

- borderColor
- highlightColor
- shadowColor
- borderCapColor
- shadowCapColor
- borderCapColor

DO OR DIE:

> > Change the color (not the shape) of parts of a single component instance.

> > Change the color of only some, not all, parts.

> > Use component.setStyle().

> > Use style objects and styleName.

Table 11.1 Styles Available in ActionScript

STYLE	DESCRIPTION
backgroundColor	The background of the component. Not all components have a background. This style works on TextArea, TextInput, Accordion (if you haven't loaded it with any movie clips yet), and DataGrid. backgroundColor doesn't affect Button, Checkbox, Label, MenuBar (but it works on Menu), Alert, or RadioButton. `dateChooser.setStyle("backgroundColor", 0xFF0000);`
borderColor	The black section of the default 3D border or the color section of a 2D border. borderColor doesn't affect Button, Checkbox, Label, ComboBox, MenuBar, or RadioButton. `dateChooser.setStyle("borderColor", 0xFF0000);`

borderStyle	Doesn't affect Button, Label, or DateChooser. Possible values are
	
	`"none"` (can get some weird effects with this one)
	`"inset"`
	`"outset"`
	`"solid"` (default)
	`combo.setStyle("borderStyle", "inset");`

buttonColor	The big face area of a button along with a section of the 3D border. The default is 0xEFEFEF.
	
	`submit_btn.setStyle("buttonColor", 0xFF0000);`
	
	This works when you use the Sample theme, but has no effect in Halo.
	    According to the documentation, the only styles that do anything with a button component in Halo are themeColor, color, fontFamily, fontSize, fontStyle, and fontWeight.
	    The documentation also says disabledColor affects Buttons, but it works only in the Sample theme, not in Halo.

color	The color of the text on the component. Works on any component with text, such as Button, Label, RadioButton, and DateChooser. The text in TextInput and TextArea is treated separately using setTextFormat() and setNewTextFormat(). `checkbox.setStyle("color", 0xff0000);`
disabledColor	The disabled color for text. The default color is 0x848384 (dark gray). `dateChooser.setStyle("disabledColor", 0xFF0000);` For Buttons, this only works when you use the Sample theme, not Halo.

STYLE	DESCRIPTION
fontFamily	The font name for text. The default value is _sans. This works as expected on components with text, including Label, Button, and Checkbox. `test_btn.setStyle("fontFamily", "garamond");`
fontSize	The point size (not pixel size) for the font. The default value is 10. This works as expected on components with text, including DateChooser, RadioButton, and NumericStepper. `test_btn.setStyle("fontSize", "20");`
fontStyle	The font style: either "normal" or "italic". The default value is "normal". This works as expected on components with text, including Label, Button, and Checkbox. `dateField.setStyle("fontStyle", "italic");`
fontWeight	The font weight: either "normal" or "bold". The default value is "normal". This works as expected on components with text, including DateChooser, RadioButton, and NumericStepper. `dateField.setStyle("fontWeight", "bold");`
marginLeft	A number indicating the left margin for text. The default value is 0. This has an effect on components with text, like TextInput, TextArea, Checkbox, and RadioButton. This setting has no effect if the text is right aligned. `textarea_txta.setStyle("marginLeft", "5");`
marginRight	A number indicating the right margin for text. The default value is 0. This has an effect on components with text, like TextInput, TextArea, Checkbox, and RadioButton. This setting has no effect if the text is left aligned (which is the default). `checkbox.setStyle("marginRight", "10");`
scrollTrackColor	The scroll track for a scroll bar. That is, the bar the scroll button moves up and down (or side to side) on. The default value is 0xEFEEEF (light gray). `textArea.setStyle("scrollTrackColor", 0xFF0000);` Doesn't work in the Halo theme, but works in the Sample theme.
shadowColor	The bottom section of the 3D border. The default value is 0x848384 (dark gray). This affects the purely rectangular components, like TextInput, TextArea, List, DataGrid, and DateField. It doesn't affect Button, CheckBox, or RadioButton. `text_txt.setStyle("shadowColor", 0xff0000);`

Continued on next page

68

STYLE	DESCRIPTION
symbolBackgroundColor	The background color of checkboxes and radio buttons. The default value is 0xFFFFFF (white). Doesn't work in the Halo theme, but works in the Sample theme.
symbolBackground-DisabledColor	The background color of checkboxes and radio buttons when disabled. The default value is 0xEFEEEF (light gray). Doesn't work in the Halo theme, but works in the Sample theme.
symbolBackground-PressedColor	The background color of checkboxes and radio buttons when pressed. The default value is 0xFFFFFF (white). Doesn't work in the Halo theme, but works in the Sample theme.
symbolColor	The check mark of a checkbox or the dot of a radio button. The default value is 0x000000 (black). Doesn't work in the Halo theme, but works in the Sample theme.
symbolDisabledColor	The disabled check mark or radio button dot color. The default value is 0x848384 (dark gray). Doesn't work in the Halo theme, but works in the Sample theme.
textAlign	The text alignment: either "left", "right", or "center". The default value is "left". It's like right and left justification in Microsoft Word. Works for components with text in them, like TextArea and TextInput. `textarea_txta.setStyle("textAlign", "right");`
textDecoration	The text decoration: either "none" or "underline". The default value is "none". You might recognize this from a:hover in your CSS stylesheets (if not, ignore that comment). `textarea_txta.setStyle("textDecoration", "underline");`
textIndent	Amount the first line of text is indented, like a paragraph in a book. The default value is 0. `textarea_txta.setStyle("textIndent", "5");`

For a mostly accurate illustration of how these styles affect your rectangle, check out the hidden chunk of documentation at http://livedocs.macromedia.com/flash/mx2004/main/04_co471.htm.

"Cap" in the preceding list refers to the sides of the rectangle in question. The tricky thing is, depending on whether the rectangle's borderStyle is "inset" or "outset", the shadow and highlight can be on the top or bottom. Caps are the ends of a rectangle. Class treats it as two caps and a stretchable middle.

Style Objects

Essentially, style objects are just a collection of style properties, like a stylesheet in Cascading Style Sheets, if you're used to HTML. Once you have this collection of styles (font family is this, text color is that), you can apply that set of styles to individual components, like so:

```
// create the style object
var styleObj = new mx.styles.CSSStyleDeclaration;

// set the styles
styleObj.fontFamily = "verdana";
styleObj.fontSize = 15;
styleObj.fontWeight = "bold";
styleObj.color = 0x336699;
styleObj.setStyle("themeColor", 0xE1F412);

// stick the style object into _global.styles, so it'll have
// an effect when components use it
styleObj.styleName = "boldStyle";
_global.styles.boldStyle = styleObj;

// assign the style object to a couple components
aButton.setStyle("styleName", "boldStyle");
someLabel.setStyle("styleName", "boldStyle");
```

See that first CSSStyleDeclaration line? With it, we're creating an object called styleObj, and it's a bunch of style rules. That's all it really means: "Get this object ready to hold style properties!"

Then, we go ahead and cram styles into styleObj. Note that in order to use themeColor, we had to use the setStyle() method. That's just the way it is.

Now, we have this style object floating around in the digital ether, not tied to anything. It's information without any meaning. It's like me walking up to you and yelling, "RIGHT!!" It doesn't mean much. We have to put the object someplace where the information will have some meaning, and that's in _global.styles. Aha! Now this style information will affect a component when called, which is what we do next. I know the "styleName" thing is a little weird, but that's how you assign a style object to a component—you have to give the object a name and then set the styles using that name.

FAQ

Tom Asks Why

Why would you ever bother with creating style objects? Because it can save time. If you have some styles that you want to apply to some components, but not to all of them, then you can specify those styles once, stick them in a style object, and tell all those components to look at the single style object. Otherwise, your code would look like this:

```
aButton.fontFamily = "verdana";
aButton.fontSize = 15;
aButton.fontWeight = "bold";
aButton.color = 0x336699;
aButton.setStyle("themeColor", 0xE1F412);

someLabel.fontFamily = "verdana";
someLabel.fontSize = 15;
someLabel.fontWeight = "bold";
someLabel.color = 0x336699;
someLabel.setStyle("themeColor", 0xE1F412);
```

With two components, it's no big deal, but if you had, say, 20, then it would be a pain in butt to change all of them if you decided you needed a slightly darker shade of blue or a smaller font size.

MenuBar Misguiding

Now, you might hear something here and there about the following being style properties for the `MenuBar` component:

- `MenuBarBackRight`
- `MenuBarBackMiddle`
- `MenuBarBackLeft`

These aren't actually styles, so trying to set them won't do a darn thing. They look like styles, but they aren't. People are misled because in the class definition `MenuBar.as`, there are three lines:

```
var menuBarBackLeftName:String =
    "MenuBarBackLeft";
var menuBarBackRightName:String =
    "MenuBarBackRight";
var menuBarBackMiddleName:String =
    "MenuBarBackMiddle";
```

This has caused a few people to say, "Aha! Hidden style properties!" Not really. These are linkage ID names for movie clips that Flash uses to build the `MenuBar`.

How do I know about the `MenuBar` thing? Because further down in `MenuBar.as` are these lines:

```
createEmptyMovieClip("background_mc", 0);
background_mc.createObject(menuBarBackLeftName, "bckLeft", 1);
background_mc.createObject(menuBarBackRightName, "bckRight", 2);
background_mc.createObject(menuBarBackMiddleName, "bckCenter", 3);
```

The `createObject()` method creates a subobject of an object (beyond the scope of this little book), so we're looking at the names of movie clips, not style properties.

You can also see that those properties aren't listed in `Classes/mx/skins/halo/Defaults.as`.

12

Setting Styles on a Certain Type of Component

 etting for all of a certain kind of component:

```
_global.styles.ComboBox = new
mx.styles.CSSStyleDeclaration();
_global.styles.ComboBox.setStyle("backgroundColor",
  "0xFFCC00");
```

DO OR DIE:

> > Set styles on a type of component (say, all checkboxes).

> > Use `_global.styles` to set styles on all components in a movie.

Yeah. Getting a little fancy here. NOTE: We have to drag an instance of the ComboBox component to the stage before this'll work.

If you don't want to write "`_global.styles.ComboBox`" a bunch, here's a shortcut:

```
c = _global.styles.ComboBox = new mx.styles.CSSStyleDeclaration();
c.setStyle("backgroundColor","0xFFCC00");
```

Huh?

CSSStyleDeclaration defines a set of style rules. The first line creates a CSSStyleDeclaration object and associates it with **ComboBox**. Since we have **ComboBox** in our Library, Flash can say, "Aha! Here's a set of style rules that

Why do we use _global? Why can't we just use ComboBox.setStyle()**? Simple answer: ActionScript doesn't work that way. When we set styles on components that we want to apply over the whole movie, we use** _global.styles**. That's actually the job of** _global.styles**—that's its purpose in life: to set global styles for components.**

applies to **ComboBox** (which I see in the Library)." So, when we set a style on **ComboBox**, it immediately is applied to all instances of **ComboBox** in our movie.

To state it in a different way,

- In order to set component styles across your whole movie, you have to use _global.something.
- In order to set component styles on a particular kind of component, you have to create a CSSStyleDeclaration object inside _global.styles:

  _global.styles.ComboBox = new mx.styles.CSSStyleDeclaration();

- Make sure that component is in your Library.
- You're then free to set the styles:

  _global.styles.ComboBox.setStyle("backgroundColor","0xFFCC00");

You saw this in the last topic, but I'll repeat it here so you don't have to flip around.

Table 12.1 lists the styles you can use. Note that some of them require that you use the Sample theme—some of them have no effect in Halo.

Those Darn Buttons

Here are the only styles that have any effect on **Button** components in the Halo theme:

- themeColor
- color
- disabledColor
- fontFamily
- fontSize
- fontStyle
- fontWeight

Table 12.1 Styles Available in ActionScript

STYLE	DESCRIPTION

backgroundColor	The background of the component. Not all components have a background. This style works on TextArea, TextInput, Accordion (if you haven't loaded it with any movie clips yet), and DataGrid.
	
	    backgroundColor doesn't affect Button, Checkbox, Label, MenuBar (but it works on Menu), Alert, or RadioButton.
	
	`dateChooser.setStyle("backgroundColor", 0xFF0000);`
	
	To make the background transparent:
	
	`_global.styles.TextArea.setStyle("backgroundColor", undefined);`
	
	or
	
	`_global.styles.TextArea.setStyle("backgroundColor", "none");`

borderColor	The black section of the default 3D border or the color section of a 2D border. borderColor doesn't affect Button, Checkbox, Label, ComboBox, MenuBar, or RadioButton. `dateChooser.setStyle("borderColor", 0xFF0000);`
borderStyle	borderStyle doesn't affect Button, Label, or DateChooser. Possible values are "none" (can get some weird effects with this one) "inset" "outset" "solid" (default) `combo.setStyle("borderStyle", "inset");`

buttonColor	The big face area of a button along with a section of the 3D border. The default is 0xEFEFEF.
	
	`submit_btn.setStyle("buttonColor", 0xFF0000);`
	
	This works when you use the Sample theme, but has no effect in Halo.
	    According to the documentation, the only styles that do anything with a button component in Halo are themeColor, color, fontFamily, fontSize, fontSyle, and fontWeight.
	    The documentation also says disabledColor affects Buttons, but it works only in the Sample theme, not in Halo.

color	The color of the text on the component. Works on any component with text, such as Button, Label, RadioButton, and DateChooser. The text in TextInput and TextArea is treated separately using setTextFormat() and setNewTextFormat(). `checkbox.setStyle("color", 0xff0000);`

Continued on next page

Table 12.1 Continued

STYLE	DESCRIPTION
disabledColor	The disabled color for text. The default color is 0x848384 (dark gray). `dateChooser.setStyle("disabledColor", 0xFF0000);` For Buttons, this only works when you use the Sample theme, not Halo.
fontFamily	The font name for text. The default value is _sans. This works as expected on components with text, including Label, Button, and Checkbox. `test_btn.setStyle("fontFamily", "garamond");`
fontSize	The point size (not pixel size) for the font. The default value is 10. This works as expected on components with text, including DateChooser, RadioButton, and NumericStepper. `test_btn.setStyle("fontSize", "20");`
fontStyle	The font style: either "normal" or "italic". The default value is "normal". This works as expected on components with text, including Label, Button, and Checkbox. `dateField.setStyle("fontStyle", "italic");`
fontWeight	The font weight: either "normal" or "bold". The default value is "normal". This works as expected on components with text, including DateChooser, RadioButton, and NumericStepper. `dateField.setStyle("fontWeight", "bold");`
marginLeft	A number indicating the left margin for text. The default value is 0. This has an effect on components with text, like TextInput, TextArea, Checkbox, and RadioButton. This setting doesn't have any effect if the text is right aligned. `textarea_txta.setStyle("marginLeft", "5");`
marginRight	A number indicating the right margin for text. The default value is 0. This has an effect on components with text, like TextInput, TextArea, Checkbox, and RadioButton. This setting has no effect if the text is left aligned (which is the default). `checkbox.setStyle("marginRight", "10");`
scrollTrackColor	This style is a another doesn't-work clunker, just like buttonColor and symbolColor. Them's the breaks.
shadowColor	The bottom section of the 3 border. The default value is 0x848384 (dark gray). This affects the purely rectangular components, like TextInput, TextArea, List, DataGrid, and DateField. It doesn't affect Button, CheckBox, or RadioButton. `text_txt.setStyle("shadowColor", 0xff0000);`

Table 12.1 Continued

STYLE	DESCRIPTION
symbolBackgroundColor	The background color of checkboxes and radio buttons. The default value is 0xFFFFFF (white). Doesn't work in the Halo theme, but works in the Sample theme.
symbolBackground-DisabledColor	The background color of checkboxes and radio buttons when disabled. The default value is 0xEFEEEF (light gray). Doesn't work in the Halo theme, but works in the Sample theme.
symbolBackground-PressedColor	The background color of checkboxes and radio buttons when pressed. The default value is 0xFFFFFF (white). Doesn't work in the Halo theme, but works in the Sample theme.
symbolColor	The check mark of a checkbox or the dot of a radio button. The default value is 0x000000 (black). Doesn't work in the Halo theme, but works in the Sample theme.
symbolDisabledColor	The disabled check mark or radio button dot color. The default value is 0x848384 (dark gray). Doesn't work in the Halo theme, but works in the Sample theme.
textAlign	The text alignment: either "left", "right", or "center". The default value is "left". It's like right and left justification in Microsoft Word. Works for components with text in them, like TextArea and TextInput. `textarea_txta.setStyle("textAlign", "right");`
textDecoration	The text decoration: either "none" or "underline". The default value is "none". You might recognize this from a:hover in your CSS stylesheets (if not, ignore that comment). `textarea_txta.setStyle("textDecoration", "underline");`
textIndent	Amount the first line of text is indented, like a paragraph in a book. The default value is 0. `textarea_txta.setStyle("textIndent", "5");`

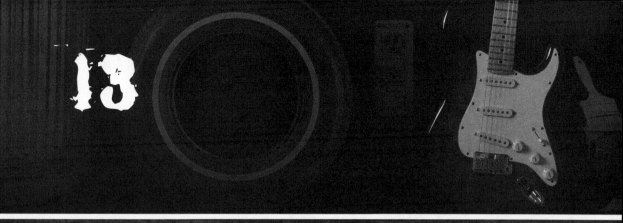

13

Setting Styles on All Components

When you want to set styles for all the components in your movie, the code looks similar to the following, which sets the text color in all your components to dark blue:

```
_global.style.setStyle("color", 0x 0800B2);
```

That's it.

Notice that it's _global.**style**, not _global.**styles**. You use **styles** when you're dealing with a certain type of component, and **style** when you're dealing with all components.

The **style** properties are the same ones used when you set styles on an individual component or a particular type of component. For example,

```
_global.style.setStyle("symbolBackgroundColor", 0xff0000);
```

works only when you use the Sample theme. It has no effect if you use Halo. (Remember, Halo is the default theme, but it's really easy to switch to Sample. See Topic 10, Setting Skins and Styles: Halo and Sample.)

DO OR DIE:

> > Use
_global.style.setStyle().

> > Control the Halo theme, which affects mouseOver- and mouseDown-type events.

Styles and Precedence

Not all style settings are created equal. For example, if you set a style, say text color, on a specific component, it takes precedence over all other style settings. In other words, if this is in your code:

```
myRadio.color = 0x999999;
```

or

```
myRadio.setStyle("color", 0x999999);
```

and later you add

```
_global.style.setStyle("color", 0x00ff00);
```

your radio button's text color remains gray and does not change to green.

The following code should clear things up a bit:

```
/*
Precedence
1. style property on instance
2. style declaration on instance
3. default class style declaration
4. _global style declaration
*/

// 1. style property on instance
//  set text color to gray
myRadio.color = 0x999999;


// 2. style declaration on instance
//  set text color to blue
var styleObj = _global.styles.verdStyle = new
    mx.styles.CSSStyleDeclaration;
styleObj.fontFamily = "verdana";
styleObj.color = 0x0000ff;
styleObj.styleName = "verdStyle";
_global.styles.verdStyle = styleObj;
myRadio.setStyle("styleName", "verdStyle");
```

```
//3. class style declaration
//  set text color to red
_global.styles.RadioButton = new mx.styles.CSSStyleDeclaration;
_global.styles.RadioButton.setStyle("color", 0xff0000);

//4. _global style declaration
//  set text color to green
_global.style.setStyle("color", 0x00ff00);
```

If you paste this code into a movie (with a radio button component called myRadio, of course), the text color stays gray.

When _global.style Doesn't Work

Just to keep things interesting, sometimes using _global.style doesn't work, even if it's the only style-setting code you have. Why? Because Macromedia, well . . . <French accent> Macromedia, she is like a woman, no? Comforting one moment, confounding the next. </French accent> *blow smoke into air outside Parisian café, momentarily overcome with ennui*

Here's the confounding part. The following code won't work on a TextArea or TextInput component:

```
_global.style.setStyle("backgroundColor", 0x00ff00);
```

These will:

```
_global.styles.TextArea.setStyle("backgroundColor", 0xff0000);
textArea.setStyle("backgroundColor", 0x00ff00);
```

So, your question, "What the Sam Hill is going on?" is answered by this: Somewhere in the compiled code of those components, TextArea and TextInput have already set those styles at level 3, class style declaration. That means that somewhere in those components, there's a line of code that looks something like this:

```
_global.styles.TextArea.setStyle("backgroundColor", 0xFFFFFF);
```

which means that when you try to change that color using

```
_global.style.setStyle("backgroundColor", 0x00ff00);
```

which is a level-4 precedence, nothing happens. The level-3 setting is still in charge.

Changing _global Dynamically

You can also change _global dynamically:

```
_global.style.setStyle("themeColor", 0x9AC54F);
colorSwitch_btn.onRelease = function()
{
    _global.style.setStyle("themeColor", 0xff0000);
}
```

I don't know why you would want to do such a thing, but I've seen a few articles on the Web that say you can't do this, so I wanted to set the record straight. You can. I just did it. So there.

Be Sparing with Your _global

It's true that changing global styles can be very processor-intensive. This is because when setting a global style, the framework iterates through all components on the Stage (in a form-based application, where all forms actually are on the Stage, this could result in many components that have to be iterated).

Therefore, it's recommended that you set global styles before any components have instantiated and never touch it again after that. _global.style is actually an instance of CSSStyleDeclaration itself. How 'bout them apples?

Skinning Components

kinning" sounds like a messy, medical thing to do, but it's the way you get precise control over the appearance of your components. Skins are the little graphics and movie clips that make up a component. Each component is composed of many skins. For example, the down arrow of the `ScrollBar` subcomponent is made up of three skins: `ScrollDownArrowDisabled`, `ScrollDownArrowUp`, and `ScrollDownArrowDown`.

DO OR DIE:

> > Dig into the theme movies that hold all the component graphics.

> > Change the movies and make your own bits.

<side>

In case you didn't read the previous few topics, you should understand the difference between setting styles on a component and skinning it.

Setting styles is done by using ActionScript to change the color of parts of a component, such as text, borders, and shadows. You can't change the shape of anything by setting styles.

Skinning is done by using Flash to alter the movie clips and graphics of an FLA file that you're using as your theme. For example, the default theme of Flash is Halo. This means that there's a file called `HaloTheme.fla`. When Flash exports your component-laden movie into an SWF file, the ActionScript in those components looks at the `HaloTheme.fla` file and pulls the components together.

</side>

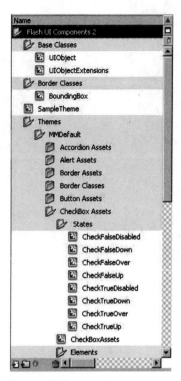

Figure 14.1
MySampleTheme's Library

Let's create our own skin. We'll start small: making the check mark of the **checkBox** component an x.

Here's how to create your own skin:

1. Open up the file `SampleTheme.fla` (in `Flash MX Professions 2004/en/FirstRun/ComponentFLA`).

2. Save it as `MySampleTheme.fla` in the same directory. You now have your own theme to play with and to do with whatever you want.

3. Open the Library and some folders. Your screen should look something like Figure 14.1, with Flash UI Components 2 as the root folder.

4. In the Library, navigate to Themes → MMDefault → CheckBox Assets → Elements.

5. Double-click `cb_check_`.

6. Zoom in. The check mark should look similar to Figure 14.2.

7. Draw guidelines around the check mark so you know the image area available for your x.

8. Delete the check mark!

9. Draw an x inside the guidelines, as in Figure 14.3.

Voila! (That's French for "Where is my wine?") You have now created your own skin.

Now you have this kickin' skin, but you need to apply it to something. Flash components use the Halo theme by default, so how do you tell Flash to use your cool new skin?

Easy.

1. Open a new file.

2. Open `MySampleTheme.fla`.

Figure 14.2
The Default Check Mark

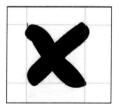

Figure 14.3
The x Replaces the Check Mark

3. Open MySampleTheme's Library.

4. Switch to the new file.

5. Drag the whole Flash UI Components 2 folder to the new file's Stage.

6. Delete it (it's in the new file's Library now).

7. Drag a few checkbox components to the new file's Stage.

8. Test the movie.

And lo, the check boxes now have x's instead of checks.

Note that we didn't really finish the job. To be thorough, we should change `cb_check_disabled` to an x as well. I'll let you do this yourself.

I strongly recommend you play with skinning for a while, because once you get comfortable with skinning, you won't hesitate to change components to be exactly what you want. It's a great moment, that dawning comprehension of "Hey, this isn't so bad." It lets you approach components boldly instead of timidly, and that's worth a lot.

Control vs. Easy

Easy: setting styles

Control: creating your own theme (skinning)

Notice we're not talking about changing the behavior of your components—that's something you can't do. The behavior is determined by a component's ActionScript, and that ActionScript is compiled into the SWC file that makes up the component. It's this ActionScript that pulls together all of the skins to make up a component, organizes them, puts them in place, and makes them do stuff.

PART III

Data

LoadVars Object

Reading in Data

Sending and Receiving Data

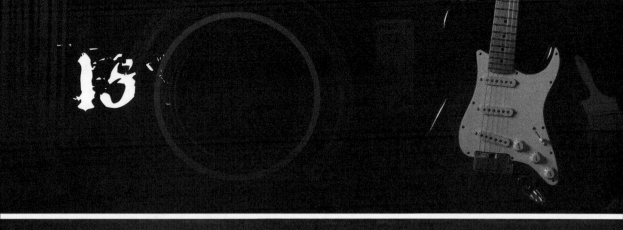

13

LoadVars Object

The **LoadVars** object is a way to package information for sending data to the outside world and getting data back. As we've seen in other topics, if you want to send, say, form information to a server-side script, you put that form information into a **LoadVars** object and then blast that data off into the Internet.

Code Fix!

Assume we've got a form with a few text fields and a ComboBox in it.

```
var addressInfo:LoadVars = new LoadVars();
addressInfo.address1 = address1_txt.text;
addressInfo.address2 = address2_txt.text;
addressInfo.state = state.selectedItem.data;
addressInfo.zip = zip_txt.text;

addressInfo.send("updateAddress.php", "_self", "POST");
```

See what's happening? First, we create a new object called **addressInfo**. We then create properties for that object and feed data into those properties. Finally, we use the **send()** method to send those variables to **updateAddress.php**.

We are not only shoving the data at updateAddress.php, but also leaving our little Flash movie going to the PHP page—that's what the _self is for. We could also use _blank to open up a new browser window.

The default is POST, and the other option is of course GET.

It may seem like a pain to have to copy all of your variables into a different object before sending them off. After all, the data just got sent automatically in Flash 5 and MX. While LoadVars takes a little more work, it forces you to be a little more organized, which I'm grateful for.

Sometimes, you just want to get information from a script or a page.

```
companyInfo = new LoadVars();
companyInfo.load("getCompanyInfo.php");

// can't assume the load() happens immediately,
// so use a function that's called only
// when the load is completed
companyInfo.onLoad = function ()
{
    status_txt.text  = "Company " + companyInfo.name
+ " data has been received";
}
```

Extra Geek

There's also an onData event that happens. Here's the process of loading: Flash gets the raw data from the server. That is, it receives the **address1=1234+Halitosis+Lane&address2=&state=CA&zip=90046** text string. At this point, the onData event is fired. Then, Flash parses that data and places it into the LoadVars object in nice little properties. Once that's completed, onLoad is fired and our little function runs.

We end up with the following:

```
my_lv.address1 = "1234 Halitosis Lane"
my_lv.address2 = ""
my_lv.state = "CA"
my_lv.zip = "90046"
```

Why would you want to use onData? What is the advantage of getting just the text string? It can be useful for some debugging to see exactly what the server is spitting out.

sendAndLoad()

The sendAndLoad() method sends data out to a file, then waits for that file to return data. Unlike with send(), the user never leaves our Flash movie.

```
sendVars = new LoadVars();
receiveData = new LoadVars();
// load sendVars data ...

sendVars.sendAndLoad("receiveAndReturnData.php", receiveData);
```

According to the LoadVars.as file, the target isn't typed because it could be LoadVars or XML. This means that you can send LoadVars to a server but get back XML. (Just make sure you use an XML object to receive the data).

For example,

```
// sending LoadVars data to a page
// and getting XML in return
var testXML:XML = new XML();
var testLV:LoadVars = new LoadVars();
testLV.gf = "Annie";

//testXML.load("gfInfo.php3");
testLV.sendAndLoad("gfInfo.php3",testXML,"POST");

testXML.onLoad = function() {
    _root.createTextField("testXML_txt", 1, 100, 100, 300, 300);
    testXML_txt.text = testXML.firstChild;
}
```

The PHP is as follows:

```
<?
    echo "<girlfriend>$gf</girlfriend>";
?>
```

Notice there's no <?xml version="1.0")?> in this XML. ActionScript can't handle it. The above code results in

```
<girlfriend>Annie</girlfriend>
```

The main difference between the LoadVars class and the XML class is that LoadVars transfers ActionScript name/value pairs rather than an XML DOM tree stored in the XML object. Otherwise, they're similar in many ways.

16

Reading in Data

f you want to bring in data from the outside world, you basically have two choices: name/value pairs or XML (note that I'm counting just pure text data here, not movies, sound, or JPEGs).

You can also send data somewhere and get some data in return. That process uses the sendAndLoad() method, and it's in the next topic.

Name/Value Pairs

Name/value pairs are just variables with values.

a=1, b=2, c=3

and so on. That's it. You get it. When you string these together, they look something like the following, which you've probably seen before as well:

a=1&b=2&c=3

The most common way to read data into an ActionScript movie is to use the `LoadVars` object and the `load()` method.

```
mydata = new LoadVars();
mydata.load("someURL.php");
myData.onLoad = function ()
{
        trace(myData.a);
}
```

`someURL.php` must output a text string that looks similar to this:

```
a=1&b=2&c=3
```

Again, name/value pairs.

ActionScript takes this text string and parses it, creating the programmer-friendly

```
mydata.a = 1
mydata.b = 2
mydata.c = 3
```

The `onLoad` function is necessary, because you can't assume that Flash was able to immediately connect to `someURL.php`, get the data, and parse it. Hitting another page takes some time, and when Flash is done parsing the data, it broadcasts a "Hey! I'm finished loading!" event (well, `onLoad` is a little more accurate). That's why you need an event handler sitting ready for when that loading is finished: until that's done, you can't do anything with the `LoadVars` object.

You can also use the old functions

- `loadVariables()`
- `loadVariablesNum()`

But you should stick with `LoadVars`, because it's more flexible and easier to use.

Loading XML

Now, if you want to load some XML into your little movie, it's a pretty similar process.

```
projectInfo = new XML();
projectInfo.load("projectXMLGenerator.php");
```

```
projectInfo.onLoad = function ()
{
    // go through XML and make sure it's what we want
}
```

You can also use

```
projectInfo.onLoad = function(success)
{
    if (success) {
        // do stuff
    } else {
        // alert user it ain't workin'
    }
}
```

The success is a Boolean (that mean it's either true or false) that reveals whether or not the XML loaded properly.

That's it for this topic. Nothing else to see here. Go back to your lives, citizens.

17

Sending and Receiving Data

getURL()

You probably already know about **getURL()** and that it's used to move the user from your Flash movie onto another Web page. But you can also send data this way by adding the ol' question mark and variables, like so:

```
// Passing information with getURL()
// Have to use the GET method this way,
// because getURL doesn't have any way to specify "POST"
// If you want to send something POST (because it's a lot
// of data or you'd prefer it not to be so visible to users),
// you should use
// LoadVars.send()
go_btn.onRelease = function () {
    getURL("getURL.php3?tiger=siberian", "_blank");
}
```

The PHP is as follows:

```
<?

    echo "Your tiger be a $tiger";

?>
```

It results in the output shown in Figure 17.1.

DO OR DIE:

> > To only send data, use getURL() and send().

> > To send and receive data, use sendAndLoad().

Figure 17.1

*Actionscript
Passing Data to
a New Page*

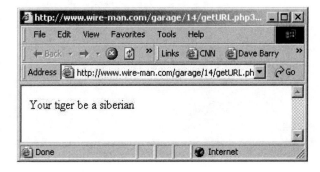

LoadVars.sendAndLoad()

To both send and receive data, you need two **LoadVars** objects: one that holds the data you want to send, and the other to receive all the data you expect to get.

```
var classID_lv:LoadVars = new LoadVars();
var isFull_lv:LoadVars = new LoadVars();

// in the real world, this value would come from somewhere else,
// like a list the user chose from
classID_lv.classid = 14;

class_btn.onRelease = function ()
{
    _root.createTextField("isFull_txt", 1, 20, 20, 200, 30);
    isFull_txt.text = "loading...";
    classID_lv.sendAndLoad("classFull.php3",isFull_lv, "POST");
}

isFull_lv.onLoad = function()
{

    if (isFull_lv.isFull)
    {
        isFull_txt.text = "Full";
    }
    else
    {
        isFull_txt.text = "Room available."
    }
}
```

```
// Ideally, of course, you'd want to provide more information,
// like how many spots are still open, or how many people are
// on the waiting list, but that's a little much for this example.
```

XML.sendAndLoad()

Really, XML.sendAndLoad() is darn similar to LoadVars.sendAndLoad().

```
// XML.sendAndLoad()
// this is really just a load() operation,
// since the receiving PHP doesn't do anything with the XML
// document we send to it

var dummy_xml:XML = new XML();
var classes_xml:XML = new XML();

getClasses_btn.onRelease = function ()
{
    _root.createTextField("classes_txt",1, 100, 100, 300, 200);
    classes_txt.multiline = true;
    classes_txt.text = "loading...";
    dummy_xml.sendAndLoad("classes.php3",classes_xml);
}

classes_xml.onLoad = function() {
    classes_txt.text = classes_xml.firstChild;
}
```

PART IV

Loading Movies
and Images

Loading and Unloading Movies

Attaching Movies

Loading JPEGs

18

Loading and Unloading Movies

he method loadMovie() is pretty simple to use:

```
this.loadMovie("whatisthatthing.swf");
```

This line of code completely replaces the current movie (this) with the new one ("whatisthatthing.swf").

Now, if you want to place an SWF into a movie clip, that's a slightly different (and often more useful) story. Say you have a movie clip called myMovieClip. You want to replace its contents with the contents of myOtherMovie.swf. Here's the code:

```
myMovieClip.loadMovie("myOtherMovie.swf")
```

Note that this usually does the same thing as the following:

```
loadMovie("myOtherMovie.swf","myMovieClip")
```

I say *usually* because sometimes it doesn't work, and it seems a little unpredictable when it works and when it doesn't (I prefer to use the first example only because it's easier for me to read and understand).

After this code executes, the myMovieClip object still exists: You can treat it like any other movie clip, manipulating its _x, _y, and _visible properties (and

101

all the others). The only difference is that that clip's contents are replaced by the contents of myOtherMovie.swf (see Figure 18.1).

The most common way to load a movie is to create an empty movie clip and place the SWF there (the movie can be easier to manipulate that way, and placing it in an empty movie clip keeps the SWF from interfering with any other movie clips you have):

```
this.createEmptyMovieClip("wormHolder_mc", 1);
this.loadMovie("whatisthatthing.swf", "wormHolder_mc");
```

Here's a bunch of code, some of which works, some of which doesn't. I've seen people try all of these and end up ripping their hair out, because all they get is Figure 18.2. So, before you go bald, refer back to this Topic and try some of the working variations.

```
//////////////////////////////////////////////////
// This loads the movie, but it doesn't play.
// Hits frame one and doesn't move
//////////////////////////////////////////////////
// _level1.wormHolder_mc.loadMovie("whatisthatthing.swf");
// this.wormHolder_mc.loadMovie("whatisthatthing.swf",1);
// this.wormHolder_mc.loadMovie("spinner2.swf",1);
// wormHolder_mc.loadMovie("whatisthatthing.swf", "_level1");
// this.loadMovie("spinner2.swf","_level2");
// loadMovie("whatisthatthing.swf", "wormHolder_mc");
// wormHolder_mc.loadMovie("whatisthatthing.swf");


/////////////////////////
// code that works:
/////////////////////////
```

Figure 18.1
That (Loaded) Thing

Figure 18.2
The Still Worm

```
// this.loadMovie("whatisthatthing.swf");
// loadMovie("whatisthatthing.swf", this);
// loadMovieNum("whatisthatthing.swf",1);
// this.loadMovie("whatisthatthing.swf","_level2");
// this.loadMovie("whatisthatthing.swf", "wormHolder_mc");
```

Loading Images

You can also load external JPEGs into your movie (not GIFs or PNGs yet, just JPEGs).

Loading directly into a level is done like this:

```
this.loadMovie("gradient.jpg","_level2");
```

Loading into a movie clip is done like this:

```
this.wormHolder_mc.loadMovie("gradient.jpg");
```

Unloading

Unloading a movie removes all of its contents from the movie clip that contains it, but leaves the empty movie clip intact.

```
// create an empty clip and load a movie into it
this.createEmptyMovieClip("wormHolder_mc", 1);
wormHolder_mc._x = 200;
this.wormHolder_mc.loadMovie("gradient.jpg");

// unloading
unload_btn.onRelease = function ()
{
    _root.wormHolder_mc.unloadMovie();
}
```

Note that you can unload a movie only if it has come into being with loadMovie(). For example, you can't create a movie clip in Flash, put some content in it, and then remove that content at runtime with unLoadMovie().

FAQ

There's also a method called loadMovieNum(). It works exactly like loadMovie() except that it loads a movie onto a specific level instead of into a movie clip.

Levels

I've mentioned levels a few times, and you probably have some understanding of what they are. In case you don't, here are some goodies:

Think of them as layers on your Flash interface. Level 0 is the bottom, level 1 is above that, and so on. You don't have to work sequentially—you can put something on level 1, then on level 1023, then on level 8, and Flash won't mind one bit.

When you put something on a level, it wipes out everything else that used to be on that level. Put something on level 0 (which is the main movie), and that wipes out everything in the whole Flash movie.

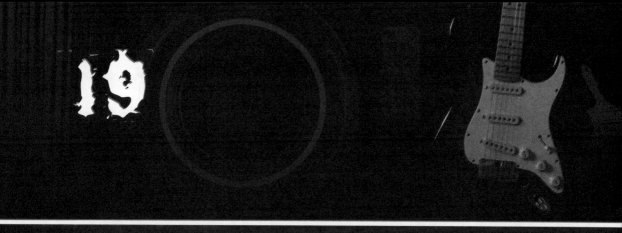

Attaching Movies

When you attach one movie clip to another, it's like attaching a third arm to the top of your head (though hopefully more useful). If you move, the arm moves with you. If you dive into the pool, the arm gets wet. Whatever you do automatically happens to the arm. The arm can do things on its own, though: It can wave without your whole body waving, or splash in a pool without your whole body getting wet.

I had some strong coffee this morning. Bear with me.

All I'm saying is that the attached movie is affected by whatever you do to the main movie. If you rotate the main movie, the attached movie rotates automatically—you don't have to tell it to. If you move the main movie, the attached movie moves as well, without having to be told.

DO OR DIE:

> > This method grabs a movie clip from your Library and attaches it to a clip that's already on your stage.

> > The two movie clips take on a parent-child relationship.

Code Fix!

```
_root.body_mc.attachMovie("head","head_mc", 15);
```

This line looks in your Library for a movie clip called **"head"** (you define that in the linkage menu, as in Figure 19.1).

Figure 19.1

*Identifying a
Movie Clip in
the Library*

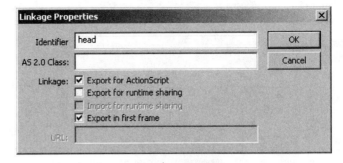

Figure 19.2

*Head on a
Body*

head_mc →

body_mc

This code takes that **head** symbol, names it **head_mc**, and attaches it to level 15 on the **body_mc** clip on the Stage. This could look something like Figure 19.2.

Whatever you do to **body_mc**, including moving, rotating, or changing _alpha, happens to **head_mc**.

FAQ

Tom Asks Why

Attaching one movie to another is something you do for convenience. For example, you can attach some instructions or explanations to a certain movie clip. Those instructions stay with that movie clip wherever it goes until you tell them to go away. It's easier to tell one movie clip what to do than to tell two movie clips.

Syntax

```
some_mc.attachMovie(symbolName, clipName, depth)
```

Where **some_mc** is the movie clip you're attaching to, **symbolName** is the movie clip you're attaching, **clipName** is the name the attached movie clip will have on the Stage, and **depth** is, well, depth. It's a number.

Big Fat Example

We're going to look at a big example using **attachMovie()**. You can download the example movie (and all the others you see in here) at www.wire-man.com/garage/. Figure 19.3 shows the completed movie.

When we first open it up, it looks like Figure 19.4.

107

Figure 19.3

Once Everything Is Attached

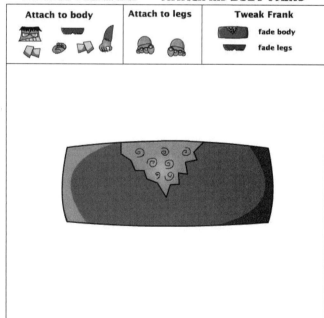

Figure 19.4

Before Attaching

Here's the goal: We start with a body, and then we attach the following items to it:

- Head
- Bolts
- Hands
- Legs

Clicking on the head attaches the head, clicking the right bolt attaches the right bolt, and so forth, as in Figure 19.5.

Once we attach the legs, we can attach the feet to the legs (each foot is a separate movie clip), as in Figure 19.6.

We also use _alpha, but we'll hit that later.

Figure 19.7 shows the library we're dealing with.

Since we're doing so much attaching, it makes sense to put all that into a single function. We'll call it position().

```
headSmall_mc.onMouseDown = function() {
    position("headSmall_mc", "head", 0,-160);
}
rightBolt_mc.onMouseDown = function() {
    position("rightBolt_mc", "rightBolt", 110,-128);
}
leftBolt_mc.onMouseDown = function() {
    position("leftBolt_mc", "leftBolt", -94,-121);
}
leftArm_mc.onMouseDown = function()  {
    position("leftArm_mc", "leftArm", -191,-17);
}
pants_mc.onMouseDown = function() {
    position("pants_mc", "legs", 0,87);
}
hand_mc.onMouseDown = function() {
    position("hand_mc", "hand", 207,-96,-22);
}
```

The position() function does a few things:

- See if the user clicked on the actual movie clip (because movieClip.onMouseDown fires if the user clicks anywhere on the Stage).
- Attach the movie clip (head, hand, etc.) to the body movie clip.
- Position the attached clip.

Figure 19.5

Attaching to the Body

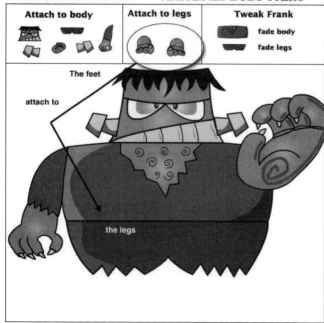

Figure 19.6

Attaching to the Legs

Figure 19.7

The Library

Here it is!

```
function position(clipName, symbolName, x, y)
{
    // see if user clicked on this image and
    // make sure it hasn't been attached already
    if (isClickInBounds(clipName) && !_root.body[clipName])
    {
        //attach the body part
        _root.body.attachMovie(symbolName,
            clipName,
            _root.body.getNextHighestDepth());

        //position the body part
        _root.body[clipName]._x = x;
        _root.body[clipName]._y = y;

        // see if a rotation parameter was passed
        if (arguments.length == 5)
        {
            _root.body[clipName]._rotation = arguments[4];
        }
    }
}

function isClickInBounds(clipName)
{
```

```
// see if user clicked on this image
bounds = _root[clipName].getBounds(_root);

// see if the user clicked inside the movie clip
if ((_root._xmouse <= bounds.xMax) &&
        (_root._xmouse >= bounds.xMin) &&
        (_root._ymouse <= bounds.yMax) &&
        (_root._ymouse >= bounds.yMin))
{
        return true;
} else {
        return false;
}
}
```

What We Did

The symbolName is the name of the movie clip in the Library, while clipName is the name of the clip that we want place on the Stage.

I cheated a bit: I added another little function called isClickInBounds() to see if the user actually clicked on the movie clip or not. The getBounds() method is the magic one here. It returns an object with four properties:

- xMin
- xMax
- yMin
- yMax

These are the edges of the movie clip in question, say, headSmall_mc. The big if statement checks out if the user's mouse click is in the same space as the movie clip.

```
if (isClickInBounds(clipName) && !_root.body[clipName])
```

The code's checking if the user clicked in the movie clip and we haven't attached the movie already. (Notice there's a difference between _root.hand and _root.body.hand. They're different clips. We're checking whether or not that clip is already attached to the body clip.)

```
_root.body.attachMovie(symbolName,
                clipName,
                _root.body.getNextHighestDepth());
```

Next, we attach the movie to `_root.body`. We choose the level via `getNextHighestDepth()` (new in MX2004). This is convenient: We don't have to keep track of where all the attached movie clips are.

Then, we position the clip:

```
//position the body part
_root.body[clipName]._x = x;
_root.body[clipName]._y = y;
```

That's it for all of the body-attached movie clips except for the hand. The hand is different—we need to rotate 22 degrees before it looks right. You may have noticed this extra number:

```
hand_mc.onMouseDown = function() {
    position("hand_mc", "hand", 207,-96,-22);
}
```

See the `-22`? None of the other function calls have it, and the parameter list in the `position` function has room for only four parameters, not five:

```
function position(clipName, symbolName, x, y)
```

But we're sending five anyway, and we handle it like this:

```
if (arguments.length == 5)
{
    _root.body[clipName]._rotation = arguments[4];
}
```

As you can guess, `arguments` is an array that contains all of the parameters passed to the function, no matter how many should have been passed.

You might have wondered why I didn't use

```
headSmall_mc.onMouseDown = position("headSmall_mc", "head", 0,-160);
```

instead of

```
headSmall_mc.onMouseDown = function() {
    position("headSmall_mc", "head", 0,-160);
}
```

Turns out, you need the `function() {...}` part in order for it to work. That's just the structure of ActionScript.

Attaching to the Legs

This is similar to attaching to the body—we use a similar, but slightly different, function.

```
rightFoot_mc.onMouseDown = function()
  {positionLegs("rightFoot_mc","rightFoot", 102,86);}
leftFoot_mc.onMouseDown = function()
  {positionLegs("leftFoot_mc","leftFoot", -68, 83);}
```

We also use the following function:

```
function positionLegs(clipName, symbolName, x, y)
{
    // see if user clicked on this image
    if (isClickInBounds(clipName))
    {
        //attach the body part
        nextDepth = _root.body.pants_mc.getNextHighestDepth();
        _root.body.pants_mc.attachMovie(symbolName,
                clipName, nextDepth);

        //position the body part
        _root.body.pants_mc[clipName]._x = x;
        _root.body.pants_mc[clipName]._y = y;
    }
}
```

Do the Fade

In order to see how parent and child clips affect each other, let's add some more functionality that does two things:

1. Change the _alpha of the **body** movie clip.
2. Change the _alpha of the **pants_mc** movie clip.

Changing the _alpha of the body (and just the body) results in Figure 19.8.

See what happens? Fade the body, and all of the movie clips attached to it are also faded (including the feet). If you fade just the legs, you get Figure 19.9.

Figure 19.8

*Fading Only
the Body*

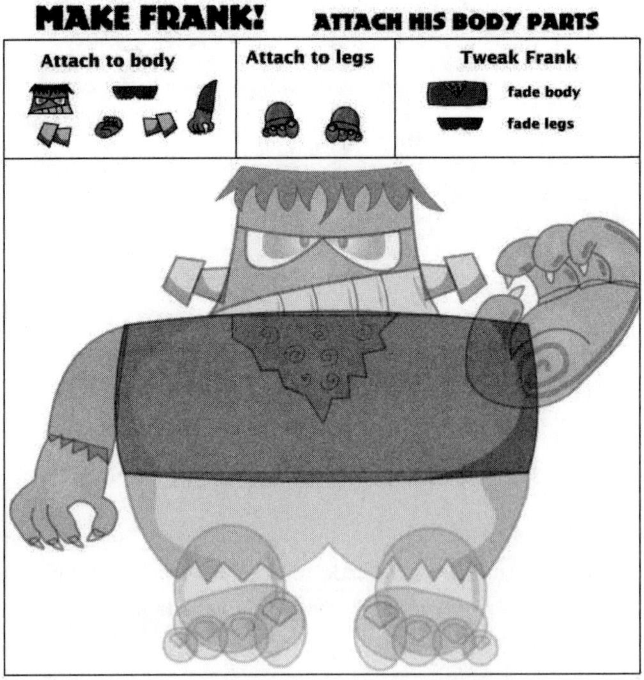

Figure 19.9

*Fading Just
the Legs*

Here's the code for it.

```
bodyFade_mc.onMouseDown = function() {fade("bodyFade_mc");}
pantsFade_mc.onMouseDown = function() {fade("pantsFade_mc");}

function fade(clipName)
{
    // see if user clicked on this image
    if (isClickInBounds(clipName))
    {
        // create name of movie clip to be affected
        if (clipName.indexOf("body") > -1)
            fullClip = _root.body;
        else
            fullClip = _root.body.pants_mc;

        // toggle the fade
        if (fullClip._alpha < 100)
            fullClip._alpha = 100;
        else
            fullClip._alpha = 30;
    }
}
```

A Little Fancy

Notice that the bolts can float in front of the head, which doesn't look quite right. To be really slick, we want the bolts to be underneath the head, all the time.

Here's the code to do it. I won't dissect it—this is already a long topic, and you're darn smart.

```
function position(clipName, symbolName, x, y)
{
    // see if user clicked on this image and
    // make sure it hasn't been attached already
    if (isClickInBounds(clipName) && !_root.body[clipName])
    {
        //attach the body part
        nextDepth = _root.body.getNextHighestDepth();

        // put the bolts behind the head
        if (clipName.indexOf("Bolt") > -1)
        {
```

```
                    // If there's already a bolt on the Stage,
                    // Make sure it's on a different level
                    boltPresent = false;
                    for (clips in _root.body)
                    {
                            if (clips.indexOf("Bolt") > -1)
                            {
                                    boltPresent = true;
                                    boltDepth = body[clips].getDepth();
                                    break;
                            }
                    }
                    // compact if statement
                    // condition ? variable = value if true : value if
                    // false
                    boltPresent ? nextDepth = boltDepth-1 : nextDepth
                        = nextDepth-100;
            }
            _root.body.attachMovie(symbolName,clipName, nextDepth);

            // position the body part
            _root.body[clipName]._x = x;
            _root.body[clipName]._y = y;

            // see if a rotation parameter was passed
            if (arguments.length == 5)
                    _root.body[clipName]._rotation = arguments[4];

    }
}
```

Loading JPEGs

'm totally going to cheat here, because loading JPEGs is exactly the same as loading SWFs:

```
this.loadMovie("bike.jpg");
```

You can refer back to Topic 18, Loading and Unloading Movies. The same information applies to loading JPEGs.

Why even include this topic? For quick reference and because it looks good in the table of contents.

PART V
XML

Reading and Parsing XML

RSS: Parse Me, You Fool

Creating an Internal XML Document

21

Reading and Parsing XML

XML used to be the Next Big Thing, and for a while, it was a Big Thing. Now? It's still big, it's very popular, but the sexiness is gone and it's just a Thing. Besides, as a developer, you're expected to be comfortable with XML. So if you aren't, what the heck are you waiting for?

Now, we could just read an XML file into a normal variable, like `myXMLTextString` or something like that. However, then we would have to figure out a way to pull information from that chunk of text. Perl is great for parsing text, Action-Script is not so much so.

Therefore, instead of loading an XML file into a regular string, we load it into an XML object. Here's what an XML object looks like:

```
var classes_xml:XML = new XML();
```

How Different Is It Really From Flash 5 or Flash MX?
Developer-wise, the XML class hasn't changed much since Flash 5. Under the hood, it's now a native object, so it's much faster than it used to be (which is good, 'cause those XML docs can get pretty darn long—XML is a "verbose" format).

That's it. We now have an XML object called `classes_xml`. Nothing is in it, but boy, is it ready. Bring on the XML! it cries.

So we bring it on:

```
classes_xml.load("classes.xml");
```

ActionScript does something darn useful here. It doesn't just slap the XML file into `classes_xml`—it parses it. This means that it takes the text of the XML file and rearranges it into separate elements and nodes, placing child nodes inside their parent nodes, putting attributes in places we can get to them, and so on.

Our XML

Here's the XML file we start with:

```
<classes>
    <class>
        <title>XML for Dogs</title>
        <availability>Full</availability>
    </class>
    <class>
        <title>Tango Fundamentals</title>
        <availability>3 spots left</availability>
    </class>
    <class>
        <title>Black Rock City Civics</title>
        <availability>20,000 spots left</availability>
    </class>
</classes>
```

Da Code

Open a new Flash movie and put this on the first frame. Make sure the `classes.xml` file is there.

```
var classes_xml:XML = new XML();

// The ignoreWhite property is super important.
// Otherwise, AS thinks that the line breaks are some
// kind of text node.
```

```
classes_xml.ignoreWhite = true;
classes_xml.load("classes.xml");
classes_xml.onLoad = function ()
{
    trace("loaded");
    trace(this.firstChild);
    trace(" ");
    trace(this.firstChild.firstChild);
    trace(" ");
    trace(this.firstChild.firstChild.firstChild);
}
```

results in

```
loaded
<classes><class><title>XML for Dogs</title><availability>
Full</availability></class><class><title>Tango
Fundamentals</title><availability>3 spots
left</availability></class><class><title>Black Rock City
Civics</title><availability>20,000 spots left</availability>
</class></classes>

<class><title>XML for
Dogs</title><availability>Full</availability></class>

<title>XML for Dogs</title>
```

Now add this inside the **onLoad** event handler:

```
var allXML = this.firstChild;
var class1 = allXML.firstChild;
var class1TitleNode = class1.firstChild;
var classTitle = class1TitleNode.firstChild;
trace(" ");
trace(classTitle);
```

You end up with this:

```
XML for Dogs
```

It's a little counterintuitive, but the text inside,

```
 <title>XML for Dogs</title>
```

is considered a node all by itself.

Attributes

Now add some attributes to the XML:

```
<classes>
    <class>
        <title level="advanced">XML for Dogs</title>
        <availability>Full</availability>
    </class>
    <class>
        <title level="beginner">Tango Fundamentals</title>
        <availability>3 spots left</availability>
    </class>
    <class>
        <title level="PlayaCitizen">Black Rock City
          Civics</title>
        <availability>20,000 spots left</availability>
    </class>
</classes>
```

And to get those attributes:

```
var allXML = this.firstChild;
var class1 = allXML.firstChild;
var class1TitleNode = class1.firstChild;
var classTitle = class1TitleNode.firstChild;
trace(" ");
trace(classTitle);
trace(class1TitleNode.attributes.level);
```

See? That wasn't too bad. Notice we don't use quotes on the level attribute.

Bad Code. Bad!

```
attributes("level")
attributes."level"
```

Looping through XML

Now let's assume we don't know how many classes there are, but we want to display them. This can easily happen when you're displaying dynamic data: You know what you're getting, but you don't know how much.

We'll use a DataGrid component to display our XML information. Open a new Flash movie and drag a DataGrid component to the Stage. Call it classes_grid and make it 400 pixels wide.

Here's the code:

```
var classes_xml:XML = new XML();

// initialize data grid
classes_grid.columnNames = ["Title", "Level", "Availability" ];

// super important
classes_xml.ignoreWhite = true;
classes_xml.load("classes_levels.xml");
classes_xml.onLoad = function ()
{
    // set some starting points
    allXML = this.firstChild;
    allClasses = allXML.childNodes;
    numClassChildren= allClasses.length;
    classNode = allXML.firstChild;

    // loop over all children
    for (i=0; i< numClassChildren; i++)
    {
        // display name of node
        titleNode = classNode.firstChild;
        classTitle = titleNode.firstChild;
        classLevel = titleNode.attributes.level;
        classAvail = titleNode.nextSibling.firstChild;

        // place into datagrid
        with (_root)
        {
            var classObj = {Title:classTitle,
                Level:classLevel,
                Availability:classAvail };
            classes_grid.addItemAt(i, classObj);
            classes_grid.spaceColumnsEqually();
        }
        classNode = classNode.nextSibling;
    }
}
```

Title	Level	Availability
XML for Dogs	advanced	Full
Tango Fundamentals	beginner	3 spots left
Black Rock City Civics	PlayaCitizen	20,000 spots left

Figure 21.1
*What's All
This Then?*

This results in something like Figure 21.1. Let's go over this section by section.

```
// set some starting points
allXML = this.firstChild;
allClasses = allXML.childNodes;
numClassChildren= allClasses.length;
classNode = allXML.firstChild;
```

To get to the XML itself, we have to look at `classes_xml.firstChild`: That's just the way ActionScript works. In the first line, we can use `this` instead of `classes_xml` because we're in an event handler called `classes_xml.onLoad`, so the code knows `this` refers to `classes_xml`.

Next, we create an array of all of the classes. The `childNodes` property is really an array of objects. Each object refers to a child element.

> *Node* is essentially another word for element. This goes back to the "parsing" we mentioned earlier. ActionScript takes the XML file, a long text string, and rearranges it into objects with properties and methods. For example, elements are all turned into objects with certain properties. If, say, that element has a child element (e.g., <classes><class>Some class</class></classes>), then that element (classes, in this example) gets a `firstChild` property, and that property is actually a whole other element.
>
> In other words, ActionScript parses XML into objects. Instead of nested elements, you have objects and child objects and such.

What is this array, really? It's an array of objects in which each object has all the information of a class element. `classNode` is simply the first `<class>` element in our XML.

Now, start looking at all the classes and pulling information from them.

```
// loop over all children
for (i=0; i< numClassChildren; i++)
{
    // display name of node
    titleNode = classNode.firstChild;
    classTitle = titleNode.firstChild;
    classLevel = titleNode.attributes.level;
    classAvail = titleNode.nextSibling.firstChild;

    // datagrid stuff

    classNode = classNode.nextSibling;
}
```

Our loop is simple enough—we're looping over an array. We then find the title node and pull information from it. For reference, remember that our XML looks something like this:

```
<class>
    <title level="advanced">XML for Dogs</title>
    <availability>Full</availability>
</class>
```

We then plop that information into the DataGrid.

```
// place into datagrid
with (_root)
{
    var classObj = {Title:classTitle, Level:classLevel,
                    Availability:classAvail };
    classes_grid.addItemAt(i, classObj);
    classes_grid.spaceColumnsEqually();
}
```

I won't go over this code because (a) this is an XML topic, and (b) you can figure it out yourself, probably.

Then—and this is really important— we move `classNode` to be the next element.

Title	Level	Availability
XML for Dogs	advanced	Full
Tango Fundamentals	beginner	3 spots left
Black Rock City Civics	PlayaCitizen	20,000 spots left

Figure 21.2

Some Tweaks, Just for the Heck of It

```
classNode = classNode.nextSibling;
```

If we don't do this, we keep looking at the first element over and over again.

Figure 21.2 shows the finished movie!

Go ahead and comment out

```
classNode = classNode.nextSibling;
```

You end up with Figure 21.3.

Also, we can alter the code so that we don't need the `nextSibling` line at all. Go ahead and comment it out. Then change the code in bold.

Title	Level	Availability
XML for Dogs	advanced	Full
XML for Dogs	advanced	Full
XML for Dogs	advanced	Full

Figure 21.3

Commenting Out the nextSibling Line

```
titleNode = allClasses[i].firstChild;
classTitle = titleNode.firstChild;
classLevel = titleNode.attributes.level;
classAvail = titleNode.nextSibling.firstChild;
```

Test the movie. Voila! Same result. Just another way of doing the same thing. Why does this work? Remember that

```
allClasses = allXML.childNodes;
```

That is, **allClasses** is an array of child elements, so we can access that array like any other.

Sometimes you'll want to know what kind of node you're looking at. In ActionScript, this means you want to know if it's a text node or not.

The way to figure this out is to use the **nodeType** property. In ActionScript, this value will be either 1 or 3: 1 = element node, 3 = text node. Those are the only two possible values.

Where do these come from? Why, from the W3C DOM spec, you big silly. Here are all of the different node types:

1. ELEMENT_NODE
2. ATTRIBUTE_NODE
3. TEXT_NODE
4. CDATA_SECTION_NODE
5. ENTITY_REFERENCE_NODE
6. ENTITY_NODE
7. PROCESSING_INSTRUCTION_NODE
8. COMMENT_NODE
9. DOCUMENT_NODE
10. DOCUMENT_TYPE_NODE
11. DOCUMENT_FRAGMENT_NODE
12. NOTATION_NODE

But remember, **nodeType** in ActionScript is either 1 or 3, nothing else.

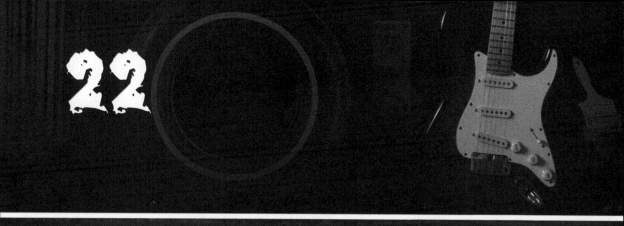

22

RSS: Parse Me, You Fool

This topic is pretty similar to the previous one, where we looked at reading and parsing XML files. RSS is just a flavor of XML, so all of the same objects, methods, and such apply. The only difference is the code that parses RSS.

When we look at an RSS file, there are a few basic things we probably want (your specific RSS reader may differ slightly):

- The feed's title
- The feed's link to its home page (not to the RSS file, but to an HTML file that displays the RSS information)
- The feed's description ("News for Dorks" or something like that)

Then, of course, you want to look at all of the items in the feed and get the same information from each item:

- Item title (or headline)
- Item link (to main story or full blog entry)
- Item description

So, that's what we want to do:

```
var myRSS:XML = new XML();
myRSS.ignoreWhite = true;
myRSS.load("scriptingnews_rss.xml");

myRSS.onLoad = function()
{
    // Get title
    titleText = getNodeByTagName(myRSS, "title").firstChild;
    descText = getNodeByTagName(myRSS, "description").firstChild;
    linkURL = getNodeByTagName(myRSS, "link").firstChild;
    _root.rss_txt.html = true;
    textForScreen = '<a href="' + linkURL + '">';
    textForScreen += titleText + "</a>";
    textForScreen += "<br><br>" + descText;
    _root.rss_txt.htmlText = textForScreen;
}
```

- **Get feed information:** The main work here is done through the getChannelNodeByName() function. When you pass this function a string, it starts at the channel node and looks for all the child elements of <channel> for elements with that same name. It then shoves all of those elements into an array.

- **Get individual item information:** We get the array of all the <item> elements, and then extract title, link, and description information from them. We slap that info into an ever-long HTML text string.

- **Display information:** When we're done looping through the item array, we're done with the RSS. We simply display the text onscreen, and voila! We're done.

How the Function Does Its Function Thing

- First, we create an array that'll hold off the desired nodes.

- Then, after making sure the RSS file even has child nodes, we assume it's valid RSS and look for <channel>.

- We set nodeSeeker as the node we're currently looking at. Note that we're only looking at immediate children of <channel>, because, well, that's all we care about.

- We start looping over all of the `<channel>`'s child nodes.
- We look for elements with the same name as the `tagName` the function was handed. If it matches, we shove (okay, push) that node into our array.
- Very important: We move `nodeSeeker` down to the next child of `<channel>`.
- When we're done, we return the array.
- All is well with the world.

23

Creating an Internal XML Document

This title's a little inaccurate: We're not creating an XML document, really, since we don't end up with a file at the end of this Topic. We're not writing anything called `availableTraining.xml` to a directory or anything. We're just creating what looks like an XML document in ActionScript.

DO OR DIE:

> > Create an empty XML object.

> > Create nodes.

> > Attach nodes to the XML object.

FAQ

Tom Asks Why

Why bother with creating internal XML documents? Because sometimes it's useful to pull in data from somewhere and structure it as an XML object. For example, I recently worked on a Charles Schwab intranet (the company has many) that read a certain directory's files and subdirectories. The job was to take that information and display it on a Web page, resembling Windows Explorer. I read the information into an XML object. Then, I went through that XML object and displayed the information in the movie. Sure, I could have jerry-rigged some way that skipped the XML step in the middle, but it was actually much easier for XML to serve as the data in the middle.

133

Basic Steps

Creating an internal XML document is pretty darn simple.

1. Create an XML object.
2. Create a bunch of nodes (which initially aren't attached to anything, but float around in the ether).
3. Attach the nodes to the XML object.

Code Fix!

```
// create XML object
var classesXML:XML = new XML();

// create classes node in classesXML
// but don't place it anywhere specific
var allClassContainer = classesXML.createElement("classes");

// add an attribute to the floating element
allClassContainer.attributes.category = "Fourth Quarter Classes";

// place the element
classesXML.appendChild(allClassContainer);

// display
trace(classesXML.firstChild);
```

What the Sam Hill?

Start with this line:

```
var allClassContainer = classesXML.createElement("classes");
```

It's pretty obvious what we're doing—we're creating an element called classes. Note the following:

- The variable that points to the element (allClassContainer points to the classes element) can have a different name than the element. That is, the classes element doesn't require that its variable is called "classes." We called it allClassContainer without any troubles.

- The classes element is in the classesXML object, but it's not anywhere specific yet. It's just kind of floating around. It's not a child node, it's not a parent node, it's nothing.

We then add an attribute in a pretty simple way:

```
allClassContainer.attributes.category = "Fourth Quarter Classes";
```

Notice we didn't have to do a `category = new Attribute()` or anything like that. Handy, I think.

Finally, we put the element into `classesXML`:

```
classesXML.appendChild(allClassContainer);
```

It may seem a little odd that we're saying `classes` is a child of `classXML`, when it's really the top tag, but that's how Flash likes its XML: The primary, or root, tag is a child of the XML object.

Test the movie and you get this:

```
<classes category="Fourth Quarter Classes" />
```

Here are some more children and attributes:

```
// first class
allClassContainer.appendChild(class1Container);
class1Container.attributes.level = "Advanced";

// second class
allClassContainer.appendChild(class2Container);
class2Container.attributes.level = "Beginner";

// third class
allClassContainer.appendChild(class3Container);
class3Container.attributes.level = "Playa Citizen";
```

Title Nodes

The text in XML is considered a separate node, which may seem odd, since text nodes don't look like normal nodes.

```
var title1Node = classesXML.createElement("title");
var title2Node = classesXML.createElement("title");
var title3Node = classesXML.createElement("title");
// note how text nodes are treated differently
var title1 = classesXML.createTextNode("XML for Dogs");
var title2 = classesXML.createTextNode("Tango Fundamentals");
var title3 = classesXML.createTextNode("Black Rock City Civics");
```

You can also write this as

```
var title1Node = classesXML.createElement("title");
var title2Node = title1Node.cloneNode(true);
var title3Node = title1Node.cloneNode(true);
// note how text nodes are treated differently
var title1 = classesXML.createTextNode("XML for Dogs");
var title2 = classesXML.createTextNode("Tango Fundamentals");
var title3 = classesXML.createTextNode("Black Rock City Civics");
```

There are a few new things here:

```
var newNode = nodeToClone.cloneNode(deep)
```

This is handy if you want to create a copy of a node instead of having to build each one from scratch. The **deep** parameter specifies whether all the children of the node-to-be-cloned are also cloned. A value of **True** means that all the children of the node are also cloned.

The following line changes the value of a text node once it has been set:

```
title2.nodeValue = "Advanced Tango";
```

PART VI

Sound

Using Simple Sound
MP3s and ActionScript

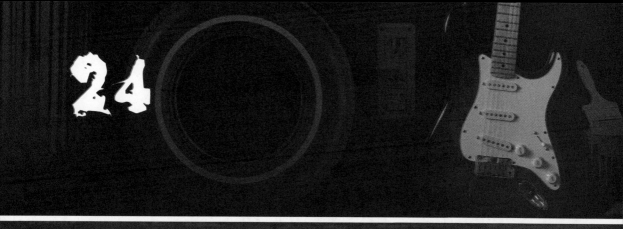

24

Using Simple Sound

Vital to Understand

One of the most important points to realize about sound objects is that you need a sound object to control a sound. You can have a sound without a sound object, but if you do, it'll just play, and you can't do anything about it. See Figure 24.1.

First

Put a sound in the Library. You have to do this through Flash, not through ActionScript.

1. File → Import to Library. Choose a sound.
2. Drag the sound clip to whatever movie you want (if you want).

Figure 24.1

Unfettered, Uncontrolled Sound in a Timeline

Code Fix!

In Figure 24.2, we have the sound in the main timeline.

```
//one way to do it
var tada:Sound = new Sound();
tada.stop();
```

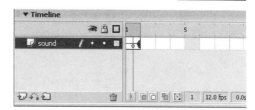

Figure 24.2

Sound in Main Timeline

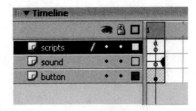

Since this sound object doesn't have a target (it could be Sound("some_mc")), this *tada* sound object controls all the sound in the movie. More descriptive code would be as follows:

```
var globalSoundControlObject:Sound = new Sound();
globalSoundControlObject.stop();
```

Now, this code doesn't work as you'd think it would. The sound in the timeline starts playing automatically, and you might think the stop(); would prevent that.

It doesn't—a little bit of the sound is played before it is stopped. In this case (the Flash movie is on my Web site: www.wire-man.com/garage), you hear the *ta* of *tada*.

The best way to deal with sound, IMHO, is to leave it off of the timeline completely.

Imagine we have a button on our movie called **sound_btn** and that we've named our sound (in the Library, not on the Stage) *tada*, as in Figure 24.3.

```
var tada2:Sound = new Sound();
tada2.attachSound("tada");

sound_btn.onPress = function()
{
    // doesn't play unless you tell it to
    _root.tada2.start();
}
```

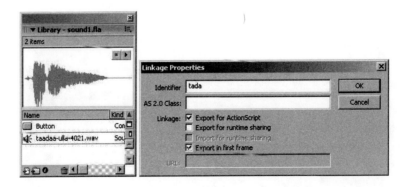

Figure 24.3

The Sound

It's also possible to place a sound within a movie clip, but you still need a sound clip to control the sound, so I prefer to keep it simple and skip the movie clip middleman.

You can get pretty fancy with the sounds:

- Get and set `Volume()`

- Get and set `Pan()` (left-right balance)

- Get and set `Transform()`—you can use `setTransform()` to play mono sounds as stereo, play stereo sounds as mono, and add interesting effects to sounds. Pretty fancy stuff for computer speakers (though I know some people whose computer sound system is the best one in the house).

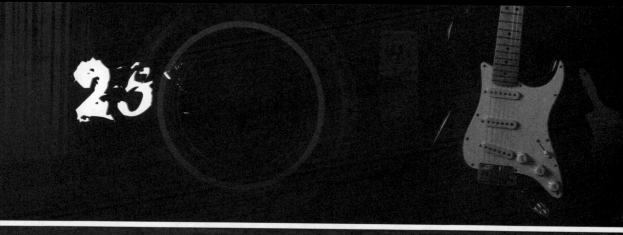

MP3s and ActionScript

 lash makes it easy to load and use an MP3 file in your movies.

DO OR DIE:

> > Use loadSound() to use MP3s files.

> > Don't forget onID3 for all your very legal song-playing.

Code Fix!

```
var frogSound:Sound = new Sound();
frogSound.loadSound("ribbit.mp3", false);
frogSound.onLoad = function()
{
    frogSound.start();
}
```

As with all other sounds, we need to create a sound object and then place a sound in it. The loadSound() method can point to a file on the Internet, like

```
frogSound.loadSound("http://www.riaa.com/stealMe/ribbit.mp3", false);
```

The false means says, "Don't stream this file." True means (duh) "Stream this file."

We use an onLoad event handler because we don't know how long the file will take to load and can't assume it happens immediately.

Note that playing sounds requires start(), not play(); play() is for movies.

onSoundComplete

There's also a handy event handler called onSoundComplete, which lets you execute a chunk of code whenever the sound finishes playing.

```
frogSound.onSoundComplete = function()
{
    trace("Was that you?");
}
```

ID3

MP3 files can have little ID3 tags embedded in them, which provide information about the files (usually song data, such as artist and title). To get at these properties, code something like this:

```
composer_txt.text = frogSound.id3.TCOM;
```

Check out the documentation for all of the ID3 tags you can check for. There are a few dozen of them.

onID3

If you're not 100 percent sure that an MP3 file has ID3 information, you can use the onID3 event handler. This event fires when Flash discovers ID3 data in an MP3 file.

```
frogSound.onID3 = function()
{
   for( var prop in frogSound.id3 )
{
    trace( prop + " : "+ frogSound.id3[prop] );
   }
}
```

attachSound()

You can also load an MP3 sound into your movie using attachSound() if the MP3 file is already in your library.

FRIDGE

Chai Espresso

Sprinkle some cinnamon and a pinch of cardamom in the espresso grounds.
 Brew as usual.
 Yum.

PART VII

Video

Using Imported Video

Video

26

Using Imported Video

Let's look at importing an MPG video file into Flash and putting that file in a movie. Flash can import other kinds of video, like AVI and QuickTime, which can then be exported to FLV (FLV files can be placed in the Library and attached using `attachVideo()`).

First, we have to get that file into the Library: File → Import → to Library.

Open the video import wizard. Choose compression according to probable user's bandwidth (dial-up modem, DSL, etc.).

Choose an MPG file. Import the mother. That file is now a part of your Flash movie.

Video is easiest to deal with when it's in a movie clip, so create a new symbol and call it `videoHolder_mc`. Drag the movie clip to this clip. It should look something like Figure 26.1.

DO OR DIE:

➤ ➤ Place some video in a movie clip, and put that clip into your movie.

➤ ➤ Control the video by controlling the movie clip.

Controlling the Clip

Let's use buttons to start and stop the movie (you can do this via the Media component). Drag a couple buttons to the main scene, as in Figure 26.2.

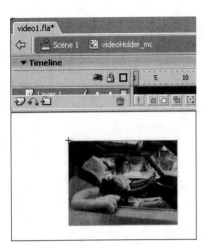

Figure 26.1
*The Video
and the Clip*

Figure 26.2
The Buttons

Call them `play_btn` and `pause_btn`.

```
play_btn.onRelease = function()
{
    videoHolder_mc.play();
}

pause_btn.onRelease = function ()
{
    videoHolder_mc.stop();
}
```

It's pretty easy to see what's going on here. What may seem odd is that you're dealing with the movie clip, not the embedded video clip directly. In fact, we didn't even give the video clip a name. How does this work? Figure 26.3 offers a hint.

The movie clip extends itself so that each frame corresponds to a frame in the movie. So, by telling the movie clip to start and stop, we're controlling the video.

Question: can you control the video directly using:

```
videoHolder_mc.muppet_video.play();
```

or

```
videoHolder_mc.muppet_video.stop();
```

Nope. The `Video` class doesn't have any `play()` or `stop()` methods. You have to go through the movie clip (or Media component).

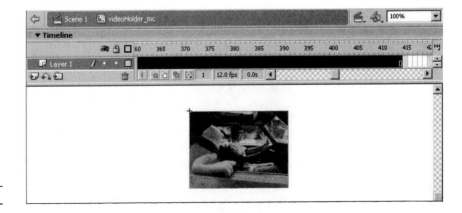

Figure 26.3
Timeline

Exporting FLV Files

As a side note, you can also export videos into FLV files from Flash.

1. Import video to Library.
2. In the Library, right-click the video and choose Properties.
3. Click Export.
4. Under *Save as type:*, the only option is Macromedia Flash Video (.flv).

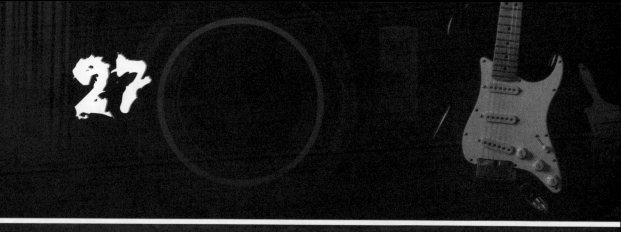

Video

dvantages of using an external video clip include the following:

- It can be edited independently of the SWF file.
- It can be downloaded as it plays.
- It can play at a different frame rate than the SWF file.

Being able to play external video files is new to Flash MX 2004. Flash MX could load and play external movie clips only with the help of Flash Comm Server. Bleah.

However, there's a catch: These external clips have to be converted into a special format called FLV. Using just .mpg or .mov won't work.

How do you get an FLV file? First, import the file into Flash. File → Import → Import to Library.

Once the file is in the Library, right-click or control-click the video and choose Properties. You should then see the dialog box shown in Figure 27.1.

Click Export, and Flash exports the file in FLV format.

Figure 27.1

*Getting Ready
To Export*

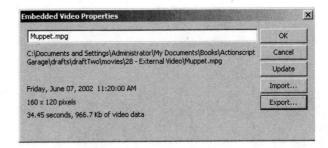

Playback Using Media Components

The easiest way to deal with external movie clips is to place a media component in your Flash movie and load the external file into that component. To do this, open the Components palette and drag a `MediaPlayback` component on your Stage. Call it `muppetMedia`.

On frame 1, enter this:

```
muppetMedia.setMedia("muppet.flv", "FLV");
muppetMedia.controllerPolicy = "on";
```

That's it! Test the movie. It'll look something like Figure 27.2.

One nice thing: It's quick to test because Flash streams the movie.

So What's Going On?

The `setMedia()` method simply tells the media component where the file to load is. The second parameter can be `FLV` or `MP3`. The `controllerPolicy` determines whether to show the `MediaController` subcomponent (that is, the play button, volume control, and such).

You can also set this to auto or off instead of on.

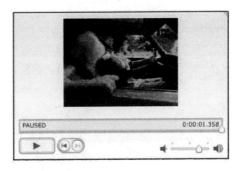

Figure 27.2

*Media Control
of the Movie*

Skipping the Component

If you want to forgo the component (which, in this case, doesn't save you anything on file size), you can do it with a chunk of extra code. Here's how to do it.

1. Open a new Flash movie.

2. In the Library, select New Video from the Library options menu (Figure 27.3). This creates a video object in the library (Figure 27.4).

3. Drag this video object to the stage and call it `muppet_video`. This video object is now ready to connect to and play a video.

4. Drag a `TextArea` component to the Stage and call it `status`. We'll be displaying information about the video in it.

5. Enter the following in the first frame:

```
// Create a NetConnection object:
var netConn:NetConnection = new NetConnection();


// Create a local streaming connection:
netConn.connect(null);


// Create a NetStream object and define an onStatus()
// function:
var netStream:NetStream = new NetStream(netConn);
netStream.onStatus = function(infoObject)
{
    status.text += "Status (NetStream)";
    status.text += "Level: "+infoObject.level;
    status.text += "Code: "+infoObject.code;
};


// Attach the NetStream video feed to the
// Video object:
muppet_video.attachVideo(netStream);


// Set the buffer time:
netStream.setBufferTime(5);


// Being playing the FLV file:
netStream.play("muppet.flv");
```

Figure 27.3

Library Options Menu

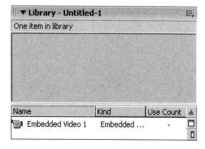

Figure 27.4

One Video Object in Library

What the Sam Hill?

Playing an external video file is a pretty complicated process, so it requires a good bit more code than you might expect. Start with NetConnection:

```
// Create a NetConnection object:
var netConn:NetConnection = new NetConnection();

// Create a local streaming connection:
netConn.connect(null);
```

NetConnection's purpose in life is to create a connection for playing streamed FLV files. That's the only thing it's good for right now. So, if you want to play an external video file, (a) it has to be an FLV file, and (b) you can connect to it only by using a NetConnection object.

The connect(null) just means "make the connection now." The null value doesn't mean anything—that's the only value the parameter can be.

Now that we have a connection to our video file, we have to use NetStream to control that file. That is, if we want to play or stop it, or even know where the video file is, we have to go through a NetStream object.

So, NetConnection opens the door from our movie to the video file, but we need NetStream to actually reach through the door and grab the file.

The netStream methods that actually play the movie are as follows:

```
// Attach the NetStream video feed to the Video object:
muppet_video.attachVideo(netStream);

// Set the buffer time:
netStream.setBufferTime(5);

// Being playing the FLV file:
netStream.play("muppet.flv");
```

The attachVideo() method belongs to Video, not to NetStream. This tells the video object, "Hey, play whatever that NetStream object is pointing to."

We then make sure there are five seconds of the movie in the buffer before it starts playing.

Finally, we tell the movie to start playing. Notice that we tell the NetStream object, not the Video object, to play the movie, which may seem a little backward. But all the Video object does here is connect to the NetStream object, which then does all the work.

Finally, we display little output status codes:

```
netStream.onStatus = function(infoObj)
{
    status.text += "Status (NetStream)";
    status.text += "Level: "+infoObj.level;
    status.text += "Code: "+infoObj.code;
};
```

When the NetStream object connects to the video and plays it, certain status events are fired, and when that happens, this function picks them up.

Don't forget to download the code and the movie at www.wire-man.com/garage.

Caveat

You might have some trouble playing the FLV movie once you've loaded it to your Web server. If you're using IIS, you might have to register the FLV mime type: video/x-flv.

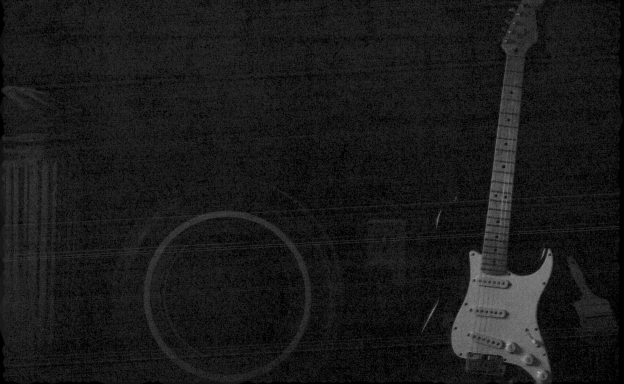

PART. VIII
Menus Components

Menu Component

MenuBar

Accordion Panel

Menu Component

L et's say you have a button, and when you press that button, a menu pops up. It would look something like Figure 28.1.

Movies never start with menus visible—the menus are always created dynamically at runtime. That is, menus are created dynamically using ActionScript.

Of course, as with all these components, you've gotta have it in the Library already, as shown in Figure 28.2.

DO OR DIE:

> > The Menu component is usually a part of something else: You click on something, and a menu pops up.

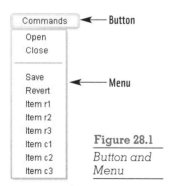

Figure 28.1
Button and Menu

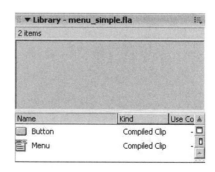

Figure 28.2
Menu Must Be in the Library

Code Fix!

Open a new file and drag a Button component to the stage. Call it command_btn. Drag a Menu component to the Stage and then delete it.

Ready? As always, onto frame 1:

```
var listener = new Object();
listener.click = function(evtObj)
{
    var button = evtObj.target;
    if(button.menu == undefined)
    {
        // Create a Menu instance and add some items
        button.menu = mx.controls.Menu.createMenu();
        button.menu.addMenuItem("Open");
        button.menu.addMenuItem("Close");
        button.menu.addMenuItem({ type:"separator" });
        button.menu.addMenuItem("Save");
        button.menu.addMenuItem("Revert");
    }
    // here's where the menu actually appears
    button.menu.show(button.x, button.y + button.height);
}
command_btn.addEventListener("click", listener);
```

What the Sam Hill?

We're checking out a few new things here at once, so don't panic.

First, look at the overall structure:

```
var listener = new Object();
listener.click = function(evtObj)
{
    // do stuff
}
command_btn.addEventListener("click", listener);
```

This is a little easier to digest, right? It's just a button with an event listener (if you need event and listener instruction, check out Topics 44 through 49). Briefly (skip ahead if you know this already), a listener is an object whose only purpose in life is to see if something happens to a piece of your movie (called an event). We also have that function, which is called an event handler, because it's code that's only fired off when a certain event happens—in this case, when the command button is clicked.

Whenever an event occurs, information about that event—where it happened, what it happened to—is encapsulated in a little event object, and that object is passed to the event handler. That's what `evtObj` is: A click event occurred, and immediately Flash created an object that contained data about the event and sent it to the event handler.

'Kay, let's look at what this function actually does.

```
var button = evtObj.target;
if(button.menu == undefined)
{
    // Create a Menu instance and add some items
    button.menu = mx.controls.Menu.createMenu();
    button.menu.addMenuItem("Open");
    button.menu.addMenuItem("Close");
    button.menu.addMenuItem({ type:"separator" });
    button.menu.addMenuItem("Save");
    button.menu.addMenuItem("Revert");
}
// here's where the menu actually appears
button.menu.show(button.x, button.y + button.height);
```

Check out the first line—that may look new to you. The target of the event is the thing that the event happens to. For example, if a button is clicked, then that button is the event's target. If a checkbox is checked, then the checkbox is the event.

We then make sure that the menu hasn't been created already (the user may have already clicked on the button, and we should only have to build this menu once, not each time the button is clicked).

Next, we create the actual menu:

<side>
Why not use _root.command_btn instead of button? Because this way, our code can be used on other buttons—it makes it more portable.
</side>

```
button.menu = mx.controls.Menu.createMenu();
```

This isn't the `attachMenu()` method you may have expected, is it? This menu now exists, but it doesn't have any items in it, nor is it even visible. Note that we're making it a child of `button`. Let's add some items to it:

```
button.menu.addMenuItem("Open");
button.menu.addMenuItem("Close");
button.menu.addMenuItem({ type:"separator" });
button.menu.addMenuItem("Save");
button.menu.addMenuItem("Revert");
```

Finally, we reveal the menu to the user:

```
button.menu.show(button.x, button.y + button.height);
```

<side>
A menuShow event is broadcast to all of the Menu instance's listeners immediately before the menu is rendered, so you can update the state of the menu items. Similarly, immediately after a Menu instance is hidden, a menuHide event is broadcast.
</side>

Types of Menu Items

Two other menu types you can use are checkbox items (items you can toggle on and off, like View → Rulers) and radio items—only one in a group can be chosen. Here's some code that adds these items to our menu (and a little something else).

```
var listener = new Object();
listener.click = function(evtObj)
{
   var button = evtObj.target;
   if(button.menu == undefined)
   {
      // Create a Menu instance and add some items
      button.menu = mx.controls.Menu.createMenu();
      button.menu.addMenuItem("Open");
      button.menu.addMenuItem("Close");
      button.menu.addMenuItem({ type:"separator" });
      button.menu.addMenuItem("Save");
      button.menu.addMenuItem("Revert");

      // doesn't result in anything that looks like a radio button
      // you have to open the menu again to see the little radio
      // button. Placing menu items in a radio group ensures that
      // only one of them is selected
      button.menu.addMenuItem({ label:"Item r1", type:"radio",
        selected:false, enabled:true, instanceName:"radioItem1",
        groupName:"myRadioGroup" } );
      button.menu.addMenuItem({ label:"Item r2", type:"radio",
        selected:false, enabled:true, instanceName:"radioItem2",
        groupName:"myRadioGroup" } );
```

```
button.menu.addMenuItem({ label:"Item r3", type:"radio",
    selected:false, enabled:true, instanceName:"radioItem3",
    groupName:"myRadioGroup" } );

// checkbox menu items can be all on or all off
button.menu.addMenuItem({ label:"Item c1", type:"check" } );
button.menu.addMenuItem({ label:"Item c2", type:"check" } );
button.menu.addMenuItem({ label:"Item c3", type:"check" } );

// Add a change-listener to catch item selections
var changeListener = new Object();
changeListener.change = function(event)
{
    var item = event.menuItem;
    trace("Item selected:  " + item.attributes.label);
}
button.menu.addEventListener("change", changeListener);
}
// here's where the menu actually appears
button.menu.show(button.x, button.y + button.height);
}
command_btn.addEventListener("click", listener);
```

The stuff in bold is new. Apologies for the unbearably boring item menu names: Item r1 and such. I think it's more important you understand what's going on with all this code.

In any case, after choosing a checkbox item and a radio item, your menu might look something like Figure 28.3.

I won't go over all the attributes (type, selected, instanceName). You can figure out what they stand for.

I hope you noticed that last bit at the bottom, where we notice what the user is doing:

```
// Add a change-listener to catch item selections
var changeListener = new Object();
changeListener.change = function(event)
{
    var item = event.menuItem;
    trace("Item selected:  " + item.attributes.label);
}
button.menu.addEventListener("change", changeListener);
```

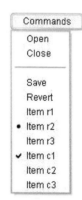

Figure 28.3

Choosing Radio and Checkbox

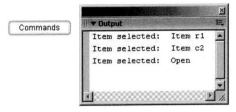

Figure 28.4

Tracking User Choices

Figure 28.5

Submenu

What the Sam Hill?

We need to know when a user chooses something on the menu, right? Not much point in having a menu otherwise.

The bit to pay attention to here is the bolded line—that's where we find out what the user clicked on. We also call the event object **event** instead of **evtObject**, because, well, there's already an object called **evtObj** in this code, and we don't want to get the two confused.

Clicking a few of the items can result in output similar to Figure 28.4.

Why isn't the menu displayed? Because the menu is hidden as soon as the user chooses an item.

Submenus

It's time to get a little fancier. How do you add submenus to get something like Figure 28.5?

```
var listener = new Object();
listener.click = function(evtObj)
{
    var button = evtObj.target;
    if(button.menu == undefined)
    {
      // Create a Menu instance and add some items
      button.menu = mx.controls.Menu.createMenu();
      button.menu.addMenuItem({label:"Open",
        instanceName:"openItem"});

      // add submenus
      var openMenuItem = button.menu.getItemAt(0);
      openMenuItem.addMenuItem("Recent");
      openMenuItem.addMenuItem("Recovered");

      // this also works
      //button.menu.openItem.addMenuItem("Recent");
      //button.menu.openItem.addMenuItem("Recovered");

      // so does this:
      // button.menu["openItem"].addMenuItem("Recent");
      // button.menu["openItem"].addMenuItem("Recovered");
```

```
      // this has no effect
      //button.menu.getItemAt(1).addMenuItem("Recovered");

      button.menu.addMenuItem({ label:"Close", instanceName:"close"} );
      button.menu.addMenuItem({ type:"separator" });
      button.menu.addMenuItem({ label:"Save", instanceName:"save"} );
      button.menu.addMenuItem({label:"Revert",instanceName:"revert"} );

      // Add a change-listener to catch item selections
      var changeListener = new Object();
      changeListener.change = function(event)
      {
         var item = event.menuItem;
         // do something on change, if you want
      }
         button.menu.addEventListener("change", changeListener);
   }
   button.menu.show(button.x, button.y + button.height);
}
command_btn.addEventListener("click", listener);
```

What the Sam Hill?

The stuff in bold is the interesting bit. Here it is again:

```
button.menu.addMenuItem({label:"Open", instanceName:"openItem"});

// add submenus
var openMenuItem = button.menu.getItemAt(0);
openMenuItem.addMenuItem("Recent");
openMenuItem.addMenuItem("Recovered");
```

All we do is treating a menu item (the first item, in this case) as if it's a separate menu. We simply add an item to it, and voila! We have a submenu. This is pretty cool automation—Flash does a lot of work behind the scenes here, which is good, because otherwise we'd have to do it.

Menus and XML

Sheesh, we're not done yet? Not a chance, my pretty. You can also build some XML and feed that directly into the menu, skipping all the **addMenuItem()** stuff.

Our finished product will look like Figure 28.6.

Figure 28.6

*Lone XML
Menu*

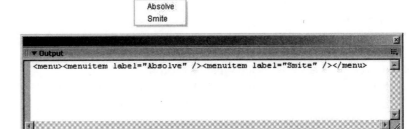

Looks a little weird, just a menu floating along, doesn't it? Well, all menus are like that. It's just their placement next to something else that makes them useful.

Here's da code:

```
// create menu via XML
var menuXML:XML = new XML();

/*
Note: The tag names of the XML nodes (menu and menuitem)
are not important; the attributes and their nesting relationships
are used in the menu.
*/
// create elements
mainmenu = menuXML.createElement("menu");
item1 = menuXML.createElement("menuitem");
item2 = menuXML.createElement("menuitem");
item1.attributes.label = "Absolve";
item2.attributes.label = "Smite";

// place elements
menuXML.appendChild(mainmenu);
mainmenu.appendChild(item1);
mainmenu.appendChild(item2);

trace(menuXML.firstChild);

// Create menu
menu = mx.controls.Menu.createMenu();

// attach XML to menu
menu.dataProvider = menuXML.firstChild;

// Display menu
menu.show(100,100);
```

Uh Huh

Pretty simple stuff, really, if you aren't spooked by creating an XML document. Just create some XML, and use that as the `dataProvider` for the Menu component. Don't forget `.firstChild`.

```
// attach XML to menu
menu.dataProvider = menuXML.firstChild;
```

Submenus and an External XML File

Holy crow! Will it never end? Let's stick our XML in a separate file and build something like Figure 28.7.

Looks familiar, right?

Let's see the ActionScript code:

```
var menuXML:XML = new XML();
menuXML.ignoreWhite = true;
menuXML.load("big_menu.xml");
menuXML.onLoad = function()
{
    command_btn.menu = mx.controls.Menu.createMenu();
    command_btn.menu.dataProvider = menuXML.firstChild;
}


var listener = new Object();
listener.click = function(evtObj)
{
    command_btn.menu.show(command_btn.x,
        command_btn.y + command_btn.height);
}
command_btn.addEventListener("click", listener);
And here's the XML
<menu>
    <menuitem label="Open" instanceName="openItem">
        <menuitem label="Recent" />
        <menuitem label="Recovered" />
    </menuitem>
    <menuitem label="Close" instanceName="close" />
    <menuitem type="separator" />
    <menuitem label="Revert" instanceName="revert" />
    <menuitem type="separator" />
```

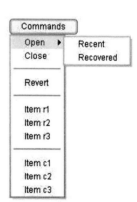

Figure 28.7

Same As Before, But XML-Based

```
      <menuitem label="Item r1" type="radio" selected="false"
        enabled="true" instanceName="radioItem1"
        groupName="myRadioGroup" />
      <menuitem label="Item r2" type="radio" selected="false"
        enabled="true" instanceName="radioItem2"
        groupName="myRadioGroup" />
      <menuitem label="Item r3" type="radio" selected="false"
        enabled="true" instanceName="radioItem3"
        groupName="myRadioGroup" />
      <menuitem type="separator" />
      <menuitem label="Item c1" type="check" />
      <menuitem label="Item c2" type="check" />
      <menuitem label="Item c3" type="check" />
</menu>
```

What the Sam Hill?

As before, the key line of code is

```
command_btn.menu.dataProvider = menuXML.firstChild;
```

This is called once the XML is properly loaded.

MenuBar

The MenuBar component is a horizontal navigation element. Figure 29.1 shows the small example we build.

This topic builds on the Menu component (Topic 28, Menu Component), so I recommend you read at least a couple of pages of it before you get much deeper into this one.

DO OR DIE:

> > MenuBar is darn similar to the Menu component.

Do It

Open a new movie, drag a MenuBar component to the stage, and call it mainMenu. It starts blank but is pretty easy to add to.

```
var menu = mainMenu.addMenu("File");
// look familiar? We're using the same methods
// as Menu.
menu.addMenuItem({label:"New",
  instanceName:"newInstance"});
menu.addMenuItem({label:"Open",
  instanceName:"openInstance"});
menu.addMenuItem({label:"Close",
  instanceName:"closeInstance"});
```

Figure 29.1

A Wee MenuBar

```
// load XML menu and attach it to this menu item
var menuXML:XML = new XML();
menuXML.ignoreWhite = true;
menuXML.load("big_menu.xml");
menuXML.onLoad = function ()
{
    var menuMore = mainMenu.addMenu("Actions");
    menuMore.dataProvider = menuXML.firstChild;
}
```

What the Sam Hill?

You add items to the MenuBar via the addMenu() method. Once you do that, you can add items to the menu that appears when the user clicks on a main menu item.

Adding the menus can happen by addMenuItem() or by pointing the dataProvider at an XML file.

Accordion Panel

ccordion contains movie clips that you can hide and show, one at a time. It looks like a kind of menu system, but since the content can be any kind of movie clip, you can do a lot with it. For example, you can create a little form with three movies in it that looks like Figure 30.1.

The Flash docs like the idea of a multipart form. (I'm not sure I agree. Such forms are usually better presented as step-by-step wizards, and allowing users to move from step 1 to 3 to 2, well, you'd better have a pretty flexible form for that. Otherwise, it would be easy to confuse users, who, remember, don't want to think—they don't want to have to figure out how to use your system.)

So, the jury's out as to the usefulness of the Accordion component, but if it solves a problem for you, great.

Populating the Accordion

The Accordion is of no use unless you have some movie clips to put in it. For our little form example, we need three clips: one for name, one for address, and one for email address. You can create these yourself or download the code from www.wire-man.com/garage.

All three of them are shown in Figure 30.2.

Figure 30.1

Form in an Accordion

Name		Name

Name ▢

Address
Email

Submit Address

Name
Address

Address ▢

Email

Submit Address

Name
Address
Email

Email ▢

Submit Address

Figure 30.2

The Three Form Movies

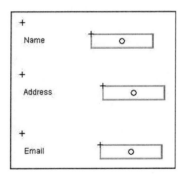

In the Linkage menus, call them **form1**, **form2**, and **form3**, as in Figure 30.3. Got it? Now, drag an accordion and a button onto the stage. Call the accordion **form_ac** and the button **ac_btn**.

Code Fix!

```
form_ac.createChild("form1_mc","form1", { label: "Name" });
form_ac.createChild("form2_mc","form2", { label: "Address" });
form_ac.createChild("form3_mc","form3", { label: "Email" });

// read data in from an accordion movie
ac_btn.onRelease = function ()
{
```

```
    nameTxt = form_ac.form1.name_txt.text;
    trace(nameTxt);
}
```

That's It?

Yep. That's it. You add movie clips to the accordion with the **createChild()** method. The syntax is

my_accord.createChild(symbolName, clipName [, initObject]);

The **initObject** can have label information, as we have, and a pointer to an icon that's displayed in the header bar.

Figure 30.3

Linkage Menu

Reading from the Accordion

Our code also has some work for the button.

```
// read data in from an accordion movie
ac_btn.onRelease = function ()
{
    nameTxt = form_ac.form1.name_txt.text;
    trace(nameTxt);
}
```

You'll want to know what the user has done in those little accordion frames, and this shows you how to get inside those little movie clips.

Reacting to Changing Movies

Sometimes you'll want to know when the user checks out a different movie in your accordion. If so, use something like this:

```
// know when the accordion changes
var formListener:Object = new Object();
formListener.change = function(evtObj)
{
    trace("now showing: " + form_ac.selectedChild);
}
form_ac.addEventListener("change", formListener);
```

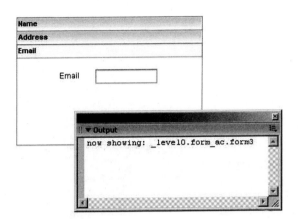

Figure 30.4

Looking at Email

What the Sam Hill?

As you do for all UI components, you need to create a listener object and attach it to your component using the `addEventListener()` method. Note that the event is called **change**, not **slide** or something more descriptive. Just little ol' **change**.

The `selectedChild` property returns the name of the movie clip currently showing, as in Figure 30.4.

PART IX

Styles and Stylesheets

Stylesheets

Stylesheets and XML

TextFormat

Stylesheets

'm hoping you know something about stylesheets already, probably from working with HTML and Cascading Style Sheets (CSS). If not, hang on!

CSS

CSS in ActionScript is somewhat limited. The properties in Table 31.1 are all you have access to.

We create a little movie that looks like Figure 31.1, with the headline in red, the location in brown, and the text in blue.

Open a movie, make a big text area (using the text tool, not a TextArea component), and call it **news_txt**. Make sure it's set to Dynamic Text.

We create a stylesheet object, load some style information into it, and then apply that object to our news text.

DO OR DIE:

> > Stylesheets work only on HTML text and XML (we look at HTML here).

> > Use a `TextField.Stylesheet` object to do your work.

> > You can also load an external CSS file (like `homepagestyles.css` or something).

Table 31.1 CSS in ActionScript

HTML	ACTIONSCRIPT
color	color
display	display
font-family	fontFamily
font-size	fontSize
font-weight	fontWeight
margin-left	marginLeft
margin-right	marginRight
text-align	textAlign
text-decoration	textDecoration

Figure 31.1

*Sample
Article
Heading*

Monster Robots Run Amok!
San Francisco, CA--Lorem ipsum.

Code Fix!

```
// Create a new style sheet object
var style_sheet = new TextField.StyleSheet();

var storyText:String = "<span class='headline'>Monster Robots Run
    Amok!</span><br>";
storyText += "<p><span class='location'>San Francisco, CA–</span>";
storyText += "Lorem ipsum.</p>"

news_txt.multiline = true;
news_txt.wordWrap = true;
// true or false, the "html" property doesn't matter here.
//news_txt.html = true;
```

```
// Load CSS file and define onLoad handler:
style_sheet.load("html_styles.css");
style_sheet.onLoad = function(ok)
{
  if (ok)
  {
    // If the style sheet loaded without error,
    // then assign it to the text object,
    // and assign the HTML text to the text field.
    news_txt.styleSheet = style_sheet;
    news_txt.text = storyText;
  }
};
```

The style information (html_styles.css) follows:

```
p {
  color: #0000FF;
  font-family: Verdana,sans-serif;
  font-size: 12px;
  display: inline;
}
.headline  {
      color: #CC0000;
      fontFamily: Verdana,sans-serif;
      fontSize: 16px;
      fontWeight: bold;
      display: inline
}

.location  {
      color: #660000;
      fontFamily: Verdana,sans-serif;
      fontSize: 10px;
      fontWeight: normal;
      display: inline
}
```

What the Sam Hill?

Right. Let's go over this.

```
var style_sheet = new TextField.StyleSheet();
```

First, we create an empty stylesheet object. The plan is to stick style information in here (font color, font size, etc.) and then apply that to some text.

```
// Create some HTML text to display
var storyText:String = "<p class='headline'>Monster Robots Run
  Amok!</p>";
storyText += "<p><span class='location'>San Francisco, CA-</span>";
storyText += "Lorem ipsum."
```

This is just creating the text for the news. Notice that we put it in a variable first, not directly into the text area. There's a reason for this, which I'll explain later.

Then, we make sure the text box can handle some long text:

```
news_txt.multiline = true;
news_txt.wordWrap = true;
```

Now we're primed to bring in some style information.

```
style_sheet.load("html_styles.css");
```

This loads everything in `html_styles.css` into `style_sheet`.

We then code an event handler that's fired when the file finishes loading:

```
style_sheet.onLoad = function(ok)
{
  if (ok)
  {
    news_txt.styleSheet = style_sheet;
    news_txt.text = storyText;
  }
};
```

If the file loaded correctly, we apply the stylesheet to the text area *before* we put the text in. Otherwise, it won't work. For example, if the following snippet was your code, your movie would look like Figure 31.2.

```
news_txt.text = storyText;
news_txt.styleSheet = style_sheet;
```

Figure 31.2

Stylesheet Comes Too Late

So, that's how you use an external stylesheet (usually easier to use and code than an internal one). If you want to use an internal one, the following code works:

```
// Create a new style sheet object
var style_sheet = new TextField.StyleSheet();

style_sheet.setStyle("p",
  { color: "#0000FF",
  fontFamily: "Verdana,sans-serif",
  fontSize: "12px",
  display: "inline" }
);
style_sheet.setStyle(".headline",
  { color: "#CC0000",
  fontFamily: "Verdana,sans-serif",
  fontSize: "16px",
  fontWeight: "bold",
  display: "inline" }
);
style_sheet.setStyle(".location",
  { color: "#660000",
  fontFamily: "Verdana,sans-serif",
  fontSize: "10px",
  fontWeight: "normal",
  display: "inline" }
);
```

Some Extra Stuff

parse() and parseCSS()

A third way is to create a string of CSS in Flash, then parse that string using parseCSS() or parse(). Here is an example:

```
var myStyle = new TextField.StyleSheet();
var copy:String = ".copy {color: #0000FF}";
myStyle.parseCSS(copy);
articles_txt.styleSheet = myStyle;

articles_txt.html = true;
articles_txt.htmlText = '<p class="copy">Click me now!!</p> Hithere!';
```

And, yes,

```
myStyle.parse(copy);
```

works just the same (only `parseCSS()` is documented).

Just FYI, here is the code for stylesheets to `TextFormat` (also undocumented):

```
var styleObj:Object  = style_sheet.getStyle(".headline");
var tf:TextFormat = style_sheet.transform(styleObj);
```

Stylesheets and XML

ere's what I'm talking about. You take some XML:

DO OR DIE:

> > You can use CSS and XML in AS (I just wanted to use a bunch of acronyms).

```
<customer>
    <lastName>Archbite</lastName>
    <firstName>Irving</firstName>
    <customerSince>2001</customerSince>
    <customerID>8675309</customerID>
</customer>
```

and you display it in your Flash movie as in Figure 32.1.

This code is the external stylesheet you use:

```
firstName {
  color: #FF0000;
  font-family: Verdana, sans-serif;
  font-size: 18px;
  font-weight: bold;
  display: inline;
}
```

Figure 32.1

Styles and XML

Archbite**Irving**20018675309

185

```
lastName {
  color: #0000FF;
  font-family: Verdana, sans-serif;
  font-size: 10px;
  font-weight: normal;
  display: inline;
}
customerSince {
  color: #00FF00;
  font-family: Verdana, sans-serif;
  font-size: 12px;
  font-weight: bold;
  display: inline;
}
cusomterID {
  color: #666666;
  font-family: Verdana, sans-serif;
  font-size: 10px;
  font-weight: normal;
  display: inline;
}
```

Notice two things in this stylesheet: (1) there are no periods in front of the names—they're not classes, and (2) `display: inline` is used for all sections.

How are the two combined? It's pretty simple.

Open a new movie, drag a TextArea component onto it, and call it `customer_txt`. Type in the two chunks of code above (or download them from www.wireman.com/garage), naming them `customer.css` and `customer.xml`.

```
//init TextArea component
customer_txt.html = true;
customer_txt.wordWrap = true;
customer_txt.multiline = true;


//load css
customerStyle = new TextField.StyleSheet();
customerStyle.load("customer.css");
customer_txt.styleSheet = customerStyle;


//load in XML
customerXML = new XML();
customerXML.ignoreWhite = true;
```

```
customerXML.load("customer.xml");
customerXML.onLoad = function(success)
{
    if(success)
        customer_txt.text = customerXML;
}
```

What the Sam Hill?

The lines in bold are what's new. Notice we set the stylesheet before we set the text—that's very important.

FRIDGE

Italian Bean and Pasta Salad

Good for those high-falutin' book club potlucks.

2 cups garbanzo beans (about 1 can)
2 cups cooked spinach rotelli (or something)
1/2 cup chopped onion
1 medium chopped tomato
1 tbs sesame seed
1/8 cup olive oil
1/8 cup lemon juice
1 ts garlic powder
1/4 ts oregano
1/4 ts basil
1/4 ts thyme
1/4 ts sea salt

Gently mix everything together. Stick it in the fridge (overnight is best) and serve cold.

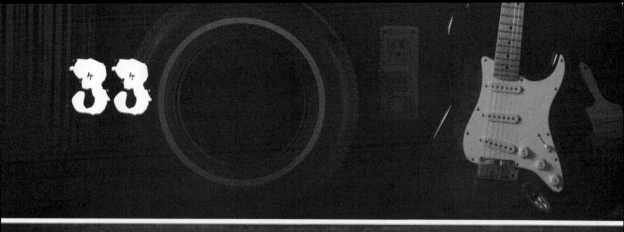

TextFormat

I f you want to change the font size, color, or other property of some text in Flash, then TextFormat is a way to go. The other option is to use stylesheets (see Topic 31, Stylesheets).

TextFormat is pretty simple to deal with because it doesn't have too many moving parts to worry about. The idea is to create a `TextFormat` object and add style information to that object. Then, you apply the style object to the text. It's almost exactly like stylesheets, except you can't load an external TextFormat file.

Start with a blank, new Flash document and enter the following in the first frame:

```
this.createTextField("ipsum_txt",1,100,100,300,200);
ipsum_txt.border = true;
ipsum_txt.multiline = true;
ipsum_txt.wordWrap = true;

ipsum_txt.text = "Lorem ipsum dolor sit amet, consectetuer
  adipiscing elit. Phasellus aliquam imperdiet lacus.";
```

Then comes the easy stuff:

```
var format_fmt:TextFormat = new TextFormat();
format_fmt.bold = true;
```

```
format_fmt.font = "Verdana,sans-serif";
ipsum_txt.setTextFormat(format_fmt);
```

and lo, you get bold Verdana text (Figure 32.1).

Let's change the order here a bit and see what happens.

```
// Now, apply style, then insert text
var format_fmt:TextFormat = new TextFormat();
format_fmt.bold = true;
format_fmt.font = "Verdana,sans-serif";
ipsum_txt.setTextFormat(format_fmt);
ipsum_txt.text = "Lorem ipsum dolor sit amet, consectetuer
  adipiscing elit. Phasellus aliquam imperdiet lacus.";
```

See how we moved the text insertion to *follow* the setTextFormat()? It looks like Figure 33.2.

How can you get around this? Sometimes, you want to add new text, so how do you apply a TextFormat object to text that hasn't been entered yet?

Easy. Use setNewTextFormat().

```
var format_fmt:TextFormat = new TextFormat();
format_fmt.bold = true;
format_fmt.font = "Verdana,sans-serif";
ipsum_txt.setNewTextFormat(format_fmt);
ipsum_txt.text = "Lorem ipsum dolor sit amet, consectetuer
  adipiscing elit. Phasellus aliquam imperdiet lacus.";
```

Check out the bold code. We used setNewTextFormat() instead of setText-Format(). This, as you may have guessed, says, "All text that appears in this text field from here on out will have this style."

Lorem ipsum dolor sit amet, consectetuer adipiscing elit. Phasellus aliquam imperdiet lacus.

Lorem ipsum dolor sit amet, consectetuer adipiscing elit. Phasellus aliquam imperdiet lacus.

Figure 33.1

Bold Text

Figure 33.2

Roman Text

This works for text that users input as well.

Note that TextFormat affects the entire text field. You can't apply a TextFormat to, say, the first half of the box and then another to the other half. Wait! I hear you cry. What if we try something like this?

```
var format1_fmt:TextFormat = new TextFormat();
var format2_fmt:TextFormat = new TextFormat();

format1_fmt.color = 0xFF0000;
format2_fmt.color = 0x0000FF;

textbox_txt.text = "lorem ipsum";
textbox_txt.setTextFormat(format1_fmt);
textbox_txt.setNewTextFormat(format2_fmt);
textbox_txt.text += " dolor sit amet";
```

We lay down some text and add a style to it. Then, we start a new style and add some text. Two different styles in one text box!

No. It doesn't work.

This is because the last line,

```
textbox_txt.text += " dolor sit amet";
```

replaces all the text in the text field instead of adding to the text that's already there. Thus, it's all new text and hence formatted by **format2_ftm**.

If you want more than one style in a text field, you're better off using stylesheets.

PART X
Random Stuff

Using Masks

Preloaders

Calling JavaScript

Date and Time

Drawing with ActionScript

_global

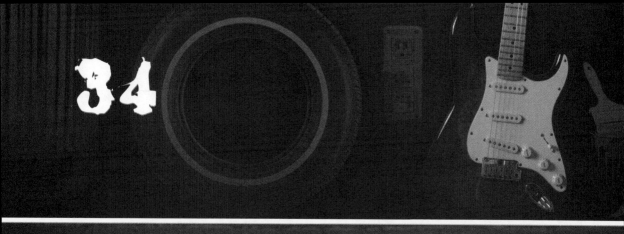

34

Using Masks

Let's go over how masking works before we dive into the code. Masking always involves two movie clips: one on top of the other. The one on top is the mask for the one underneath it.

Now, you might assume that the movie clip on top (the mask) blocks the movie beneath it, but the opposite happens. It's like the mask is a wall that blocks you from seeing anything underneath it except for the mask itself—a window that lets you look through it.

For example, Figure 34.1 is a screenshot of two shapes in a Flash movie.

Now, we make the striped oval a mask. Think about it—what will this look like? Remember, the stripes are a window through which you can see the square. See Figure 34.2.

How do you do this? Easy!

Figure 34.1
Two Simple Shapes

Figure 34.2
The Mask in Action

Code Fix!

Call the square `square_mc` and the oval `circle_mc`.

```
square_mc.setMask(circle_mc);
```

That's it. To get a better idea of how it works, add the following:

```
square_mc.onPress = function ()
{
    this.startDrag();
}
square_mc.onRelease = function ()
{
    this.stopDrag();
}
```

Play around with it a bit, and you'll get a better feel for how masks work. Now reverse it.

```
circle_mc.setMask(square_mc);
```

See how it's different? I know, it looks pretty similar, but pay attention to the colors—it's a reminder of what you're actually seeing, since the shapes are necessarily similar.

Another Example

Let's try this with shapes we create ourselves. See Figure 34.3.

Figure 34.3

The Masked Square

```
this.createEmptyMovieClip("maskMe_mc",1);

with (maskMe_mc)
{
    lineStyle(5,0x0000FF);
    moveTo(100,100);
    beginFill(0x0000FF);
    lineTo(100,300);
    lineTo(300,300);
    lineTo(300,100);
    lineTo(100,100);
    endFill();
}
```

```
this.createEmptyMovieClip("mask_mc",2);

with (mask_mc)
{
    lineStyle(5,0x000000);
    moveTo(100,100);
    beginFill(0x000000);
    lineTo(100,200);
    lineTo(200,200);
    lineTo(200,100);
    lineTo(100,100);
    endFill();
}
maskMe_mc.setMask(mask_mc);


mask_mc.onPress = function()
{
    this.startDrag();
}
mask_mc.onRelease = function ()
{
    this.stopDrag();
}
```

Preloaders

Briefly, a preloader is a little movie that plays while your big movie is loading in the background. People usually show a little progress bar in their preloader (many films in Stick Figure Death Theater do—http://www.sfdt.com—but StrongBad's email—http://www.homestarrunner.com/sbemail.html—doesn't).

Here's how to set up your movie. First, I'll show you a screenshot of the timeline in Figure 35.1, because that's easier than explaining it in excruciating detail.

In the content layer, the first two frames are taken up by a red rectangle. That's the preloader. On frame 3 is a titanic image, which should take a little while to load over the Internet (and thus give the preloader something to).

DO OR DIE:

> > There are so many preloaders available on the Internet, I'm surprised you're even looking at this topic. But good! Glad you're here.

Figure 35.1

Preloader Timeline

Code Fix!

Frame 1:

```
var totalBytes:Number = Math.round(this.getBytesTotal() / 1024);
var loadedBytes:Number = Math.round(this.getBytesLoaded() / 1024);
var percentDone:Number = Math.round((loadedBytes / totalBytes) * 100);
if (_root._framesloaded >= _root._totalframes)
{
    gotoAndPlay("start");
}
```

Frame 2:

```
this.gotoAndPlay(1);
```

Frame 3:

Add a frame label of "start".

on scale_mc:

```
onClipEvent (enterFrame)
{
    this._xscale = _root.percentDone;
}
```

I know I always harp on keeping all your code on the first frame, but I think it's fine to make an exception once in a while.

Also, of course, you can use the ProgressBar component.

ProgressBar Component

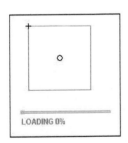

Figure 35.2

ProgressBar and Loader

The ProgressBar component is meant to be used with the Loader component, so drag a ProgressBar and a Loader component to your Stage, as in Figure 35.2.

```
// event mode
loader.autoLoad = false;
loader.contentPath =
"http://imagecache2.allposters.com/images/86/017_PP0240.jpg";
pBar.source = loader;
// loading does not start until the load method is invoked
loader.load();
```

This code results in Figure 35.3.

What the Sam Hill?

We set `autoLoad` to false, because there's nothing to automatically load—we haven't told our loader what to load yet. So, it needs to just cool its heels and not try anything yet. We'll let it know when we're ready.

Next, we specify `contentPath`, which . . . aw, heck, it's pretty darned obvious.

We call our ProgressBar `pBar` because it sounds kind of funny. ProgressBar components need to know what they're tracking—what's being loaded.

Finally, we tell our loader to start loading. It leaps into action like a Labrador retriever.

That's all you need to do, really, unless you want the completed progress bar to disappear (highly recommended):

```
loaderListen = new Object();
loaderListen.complete = function(eventObject)
{
    pBar.visible = false;
}
loader.addEventListener("complete", loaderListen)
```

Figure 35.3

Loaded Image

Preloading and Components

If you're not using the ProgressBar component, you probably have the preloader on frames 1 and 2, and the rest of the movie in frame 3. If you're using any other components, though, you have one more step to take.

Components are loaded into your movie before the first frame is rendered, which means they're loading while your preloader sits there, doing nothing useful, watching *American Idol* or something. If you don't want this to happen, you need to deselect the *Export in first frame* in the component's Linkage Properties dialog as shown in Figure 35-4.

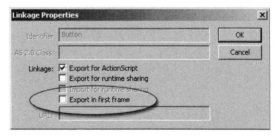

Figure 35.4

Click Here

36

Calling JavaScript

t's not too often you'll have to call JavaScript from your Flash movie. If you think you do, take another look at it. Are you sure?

You are? Fine, then.

DO OR DIE:

➤➤ fscommand() and getURL() can call JavaScript functions.

➤➤ Use getURL(). It's easier and isn't tied to Internet Explorer.

fscommand()

fscommand() is a powerful Flash function that lets you call JavaScript functions and pass messages to Macromedia Director or Visual Basic, Visual C++, and the like.

I never use it, honestly. I have trouble making it work in Firefox (the Mozilla open source browser), though it works fine in Internet Explorer. I know most of the globe is on IE, but it's a principle thing for me. I want my Web sites to work on non-Microsoft browsers.

So, if you do want to use fscommand(), the ActionScript looks something like this:

```
fscommand("alert", "Don't press that button again.");
```

You should also then publish your Flash movie with the Publish Settings template as "Flash with FSCommand," as in Figure 36.1.

Figure 36.1

FSCommand Template

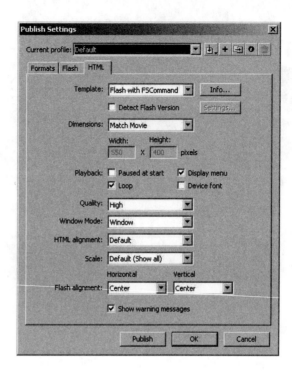

Publish your HTML page, and this comes with it:

```
<script language="JavaScript">
<!--
var isInternetExplorer = navigator.appName.indexOf("Microsoft") != -1;
// Handle all the FSCommand messages in a Flash movie.
function js1_DoFSCommand(command, args) {
    var js1Obj = isInternetExplorer ? document.all.js1 : document.js1;
    //
    // Place your code here.
    //
}
// Hook for Internet Explorer.
if (navigator.appName && navigator.appName.indexOf("Microsoft") != -1
&& navigator.userAgent.indexOf("Windows") != -1 &&
navigator.userAgent.indexOf("Windows 3.1") == -1) {
    document.write('<script language=\"VBScript\"\>\n');
    document.write('On Error Resume Next\n');
    document.write('Sub js1_FSCommand(ByVal command, ByVal args)\n');
    document.write('Call js1_DoFSCommand(command, args)\n');
```

```
    document.write('End Sub\n');
    document.write('</script\>\n');
}
//-->
</script>
```

Whoa, Nelly. Notice the bold line. The name of my Flash movie is `js1.fla`, which is where the `js1` comes from. The `alert` is passed into command, and `Don't press that button again.` is passed into `args`.

This is overkill for JavaScript, in my opinion. Here's an easier way to do it (say you have a button called `js_btn`):

```
js_btn.onPress = function ()
{
    url = "javascript:showAlert('howdy do')";
    getURL(url);
}
```

And in the HTML page, type:

```
function showAlert(ms)
{
    alert(ms);
}
```

Much simpler, no? So, for calling JavaScript functions from your Flash movie, I recommend using `getURL("javascript:something")` instead of `fscommand()`.

Date and Time

Since we're in the land of ActionScript, time is wrapped in date, so this topic is all about the **Date** object.

I assume you already know how to create something like the following without breaking into a sweat:

```
now = new Date();
```

Ready? No? Well, hang on. Let's start with a bug, because I'm in that kind of mood.

```
// you can create a nonsensical date
// without causing an error
test_date = new Date(2004, 16, 43);
```

This works just fine. If you trace it,

```
trace(test_date);
```

you end up with

```
Sun Jun 12 00:00:00 GMT-0700 2005
```

Finding How Long
From Now Until Then

Here's some code to find the number of months and days between two dates:

```
// this assumes that the two events take place in the same year.
// Or, more specifically, now is earlier than October 19, 2004.
end_date = new Date(2004, 9, 19);
now_date = new Date();

var monthsLeft:Number;
var daysLeft:Number;

// find out how many months and days are left
// between now_date and end_date

// find months left
monthsLeft = end_date.getMonth() - now_date.getMonth();
if (now_date.getDate() > free_date.getDate())
{
     monthsLeft -= 1;
}

// find days left
if (now_date.getDate() > end_date.getDate())
{
     // get number of days from now until end of the month
     var daysInMonth:Number = new Date(now_date.getYear(),
     now_date.getMonth()+1, 0).getDate();
     var daysLeftInMonth:Number = daysInMonth - now_date.getDate()
     daysLeft = end_date.getDate() + daysLeftInMonth;

}
else
{
     daysLeft = end_date.getDate() - now_date.getDate();
}

trace("monthsLeft: " + monthsLeft);
trace("daysLeft: " + daysLeft);
```

You can also get two dates via DateField components and figure out the time distance between those two random dates.

Time

What about time stuff? Gosh, it's so boring—getMinutes(), getSeconds(), getHours()—you get it. It's the same kind of thing as the date stuff, anyway.

But, since there's nothing on TV, let's just take a quick look. For time, do some **onEnterFrame** thing where it's constantly updating. All you need is a text field called clock_txt.

```
this.onEnterFrame = function() {
    var targetHour:Number = 23;
    var targetMin:Number = 60;
    var targetSec:Number = 60;

    now = new Date();
    nowHours = now.getHours();
    nowMin = now.getMinutes();
    nowSec = now.getSeconds();

    remainingHour = targetHour - nowHours;

    // I'm using -1 here so the count is from 00 to 59,
    // not 1 to 60.
    remainingMin = targetMin - nowMin - 1;
    remainingSec = targetSec - nowSec - 1;

    // Note: no curly braces here
    // This is an acceptable way to write if statements
    // as long as there's only one line of code after the
    // if statement
    if (remainingMin < 10)
        remainingMin = "0" + remainingMin;

    if (remainingSec < 10)
        remainingSec = "0" + remainingSec;

    clock_txt.text = remainingHour + " : " + remainingMin + " : " +
      remainingSec;
}
```

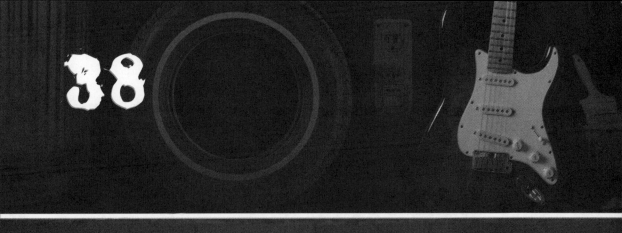

Drawing with ActionScript

ActionScript has some basic, simple ways for you to draw lines and curves, and fill them with a color. It also lets you create gradients, but that's a pretty tedious process, so we just focus on the lines and curves.

DO OR DIE:

>> You can draw lines, curves, and shapes at runtime.

>> Drawing with ActionScript is good for when you want the user to be able to bend or stretch things on the screen.

>> It is also helpful when duplicating a movie clip is too constraining.

 FAQ

Tom Asks Why

If you have a number of dynamic shapes to create (and they're pretty simple, like boxes or squares), drawing them yourself in ActionScript can be useful. Also, if you have lines that you want to change shape (say, bend one way and then the other), drawing them using ActionScript is a good, simple way to do it.

Code Fix!

Let's start with Frame 1 of a new movie:

```
this.createEmptyMovieClip("line1",1);
line1.lineStyle(5,0x0000FF,100);
line1.lineTo(300,300);
```

Figure 38.1

A Blue Diagonal Line

When you don't specify the initial starting point, it's assumed to be (0,0).

The 5 is the line thickness. 0x0000FF is the hex way of saying blue. 100 is the alpha setting: 100 is opaque (normal), 0 is transparent.

0xrrggbb is how you define color in much of ActionScript. The 0x says, "Here comes a number in hex."

The results are shown in Figure 38.1.

Drawing Shapes

Drawing shapes is really just drawing lines and adding a fill to them.

```
this.createEmptyMovieClip("line1",1);
with(line1) {
1.  lineStyle(5,0x0000FF);
2.  moveTo(400,100);
3.  beginFill(0x000000, 10);
    lineTo(300,300);
    lineTo(0,200);
4.  endFill();

    beginFill(0x0000FF, 40);
    moveTo(0,200);
    lineTo(300,0);
    lineTo(400,100);
    endFill();
}
```

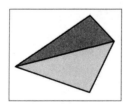

Figure 38.2

Straight Lines and a Few Fills

1. We tell ActionScript what the line will look like—we're not drawing anything yet.

2. Draw a line from (0,0) to (400,100).

3. Start filling with black. As soon as we draw something that has a bend in it, fill in everything from the start point to the end point.

4. Pull back on the paint bucket. If we drew some more lines at this point, there wouldn't be any fill between them. See Figure 38.2.

Drawing Curves

Curves are trickier (but not if you've drawn them in Photoshop or Illustrator). Curves have three points that tell Flash how to draw a curve. Two points are the start and end points of the curve (also called *anchors*). The third is a weird little beast called the control point. See Figure 38.3.

Here's the syntax:

```
my_mc.curveTo(controlX, controlY, anchorX, anchorY)
```

Here's some code (see the result in Figure 38.4):

```
this.createEmptyMovieClip("curve1",1)
with(curve1)
{
    lineStyle(5,0x0000FF);
    moveTo(100,100);
    curveTo(200,100,200,200);
    curveTo(200,300,100,300);
    curveTo(0,300,0,200);
    curveTo(0,100,100,100);
}
```

Now let's get a little fancier (see Figure 38.5):

```
this.createEmptyMovieClip("curve1",1)
with(curve1)
{
    lineStyle(5, 0x0000FF);
    moveTo(100,100);
    curveTo(200,100,200,200);
    curveTo(200,300,100,300);
    curveTo(0,300,0,200);
    curveTo(0,100,100,100);

    curveTo(150,100,200,200);
    curveTo(200,250,100,300);
    curveTo(50,300,0,200);
    curveTo(0,150,100,100);
```

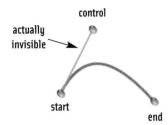

Figure 38.3

Start, End, and Control Points for a Curve

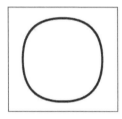

Figure 38.4

Four Curves and Very Nearly a Circle

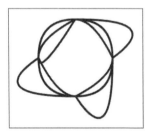

Figure 38.5

A Bunch of Different Curves

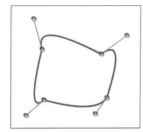

Figure 38.6

The Final Movie, with Curves and Handles

```
curveTo(350,100,200,200);
curveTo(200,450,100,300);
curveTo(-150,300,0,200);
curveTo(0,250,100,100);
}
```

Kick Butt!

Drag eight buttons and call them `anchor1`, `anchor2`, `anchor3`, `anchor4`, and `control1`, `control2`, `control3`, `control4`.

I used Window → Other Panels → Common Libraries → Buttons. The result is shown in Figure 38.6.

```
anchor1._xscale = anchor1._yscale = 50
anchor2._xscale = anchor2._yscale = 50
anchor3._xscale = anchor3._yscale = 50
anchor4._xscale = anchor4._yscale = 50
control1._xscale = control1._yscale = 50
control2._xscale = control2._yscale = 50
control3._xscale = control3._yscale = 50
control4._xscale = control4._yscale = 50

anchor1.onPress = anchor2.onPress = dragThis;
anchor3.onPress = anchor4.onPress = dragThis;
control1.onPress = control2.onPress = dragThis;
control3.onPress = control4.onPress = dragThis;

anchor1.onRelease = anchor2.onRelease = dontDragThis;
anchor3.onRelease = anchor4.onRelease = dontDragThis;
control1.onRelease = control2.onRelease = dontDragThis;
control3.onRelease = control4.onRelease = dontDragThis;

function dragThis()
{
    startDrag(this)
}

function dontDragThis()
{
    stopDrag()
}
_root.createEmptyMovieClip("curve1",1)
```

```
onEnterFrame = function ()
{
    clear()
    // draw curves
    lineStyle(5, 0x009900);
    moveTo(anchor1._x, anchor1._y)
    curveTo(control1._x, control1._y, anchor2._x, anchor2._y)
    curveTo(control2._x, control2._y, anchor3._x, anchor3._y)
    curveTo(control3._x, control3._y, anchor4._x, anchor4._y)
    curveTo(control4._x, control4._y, anchor1._x, anchor1._y)
    // draw handles
    lineStyle(3, 0xEAA755);
    moveTo(anchor1._x, anchor1._y)
    lineTo(control1._x, control1._y)
    moveTo(anchor2._x, anchor2._y)
    lineTo(control2._x, control2._y)
    moveTo(anchor3._x, anchor3._y)
    lineTo(control3._x, control3._y)
    moveTo(anchor4._x, anchor4._y)
    lineTo(control4._x, control4._y)
}
```

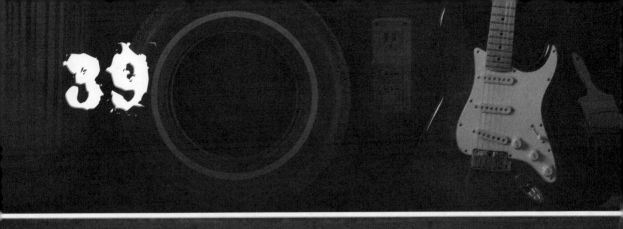

_global

U sing _global is like saying, "This variable or function is hereby placed on the highest pedestal, viewable from _root to the most nested subsymbol. Have you need, code _global, and it shall be there!"

That is, a global variable or function is viewable from all timelines and scopes in your Flash movie.

DO OR DIE:

>> Use _global to create variables or functions that every timeline can see.

Code Fix!

```
_global.speed = 70;

// changes _global.speed
speed =+ 10;

function fasterPussycat(velocity)
{
    // this "speed" is completely
    // separate from _global.speed
    // because it's defined in a
    // function
    var speed = velocity;
    speed = velocity + 10;
```

```
// how to use both?
speed += _global.speed;
    }
```

The comments explain most of this code. The fasterPussycat function (bonus points if you know the reference *without* Googling) uses both global and local variables. From any function anywhere in your movie, you can refer to _global.

You can also scope functions as global, like so:

```
_global.userAlert = function()
{
    alert("What do you think you're doing??");
}
```

That's it, essentially. You can also create global objects and classes (similar to Math and Date).

Of course, you also set styles using _global:

```
_global.style.setStyle("color", 0x669999);
```

Topic 31, Stylesheets, has more information on style.

PART XI
Classes

Classes and Objects: An Introduction

First of all, know that you may not need objects and classes in your code. They can be useful, but they don't solve all problems. Some people think object-oriented programming (OOP) is just an extended fad, and others will throw Molotov cocktails at your cat for saying that (never let it be said that programmers are an unemotional lot).

So, what the heck is an object? (If you already know, skip to some other topic—there are no surprises for you here).

Chances are you've already read some tutorials about classes and objects—they're all over the Net. Most of them say objects are like bicycles, or, in a radical twist, that they're like cars.

Bull! Forget all of that. Those explanations were totally useless and confusing to me when I was learning about objects.

Objects in code are *not like real objects*. Not at all. Not even a little bit. Just because they happen to be called objects doesn't mean that's the best way to describe them.

Code objects are more like bags, or containers. Calling an object *myObject* is like calling a bag *myBag*. It starts out empty. Then you put stuff in it. What goes in an object are

- Variables
- Functions

That's right—the plain ol' variables and functions you've been working with and writing yourself for a while. (At least, I hope so. If not, you stand a good chance of being pretty confused pretty soon).

That's it—objects are containers with variables and functions in them. Thus,

```
myObject.someVariable = whatever;
myObject.someFunction(); // does something
```

However, in Object Land, variables are called *properties* and functions are called *methods*. They're the same thing, though.

```
myObject.someProperty = whatever;
myObject.someMethod(); // does something
```

That's it.

BIG WORD: encapsulated. Because an object contains these properties and methods, it's said to *encapsulate* them. They don't exist anywhere except right in that object.

This usually also means that you can mess with the properties and methods in the object and nothing else really gets affected. What happens in the object stays in the object. (That's not 100 percent true, but it's all you need to know right now. There is plenty of time for mind-bending exceptions to the rules later. Bwah ha ha.)

Encapsulation allows a certain amount of freedom, kind of like that you can dress for an evening out on the town, but no one sees how your closet is organized.

An example of an object is `customerInfo_obj`. Properties of `customerInfo_obj` are as follows:

```
customerInfo_obj.firstName
customerInfo_obj.lastName
customerInfo_obj.age
customerInfo_obj.gender
customerInfo_obj.emailAddress
```

Methods of `customerInfo_obj` are these:

```
customerInfo_obj.spam()
customerInfo_obj.overCharge()
```

That's about it for objects. Still with me? Let's check out some classes: Classes tell an object what properties and methods it can have in it. For example, a class would say, "Lo! There shall be objects of `customerInfo`. And yea, they will have `firstName` and `lastName`, `emailAddress`, `gender`, and `age`." The code saw that this was good and thus spake: "That is not all: These objects, made in my image, shall be able to both `spam()` and `deleteCustomer()`. These are their methods. I have spoken. Spread the word."

It's more boring in actual code, but that's objects and classes, in a nutshell. As you might imagine, it can get wildly more complicated than that. So, what the heck, let's complicate things by looking at some actual code.

Actual Code

(Unbelievers, scatter yourselves! The True Code cometh!)

And the developer said, "Let there be this object." And there was that object. The other functions saw this object, that it was syntactically correct, and that it was good.

(Real code is up next in Topic 41, Your First Class.)

Your First Class

 et's create a class of some sort. We start out slow and simple, and then pick up speed.

Here's a quickie:

```
class CustomerInfo {
    // properties
    // methods
}
```

With me so far? Cool. Let's throw in a little more:

```
class CustomerInfo
{
    // properties
    var firstName:String;
    var lastName:String;
    var gender:String;
    var age:Number;
    var emailAddress:String;
```

```
    // methods
    function spam()
    {
          // do stuff
    }

    function deleteCustomer ()
    {
          //do other stuff
    }
}
```

Now, it's good we're setting the properties and methods here. However, it's not enough. We need a special function that actually creates the object.

For example, when you say

```
var customerBob:Object = new
   CustomerInfo("Bob","Roberts",34,"dude");
```

that CustomerInfo() has to be an actual function inside your class:

```
class CustomerInfo
{
    // properties
    var firstName:String;
    var lastName:String;
    var gender:String;
    var age:Number;
    var emailAddress:String;

    // constructor function
    function CustomerInfo (fName:String, lName:String, age:Number,
      boyOrGirl:String)
    {
          this.firstName = fName;
          this.lastName = lName;
          this.age = age;
          this.gender = gender;
    }

    // methods
    function spam()
```

```
    {
        // do stuff
    }

    function deleteCustomer ()
    {
        //do other stuff
    }
}
```

It may seem redundant to define the properties outside of the constructor function and then to set them again inside the function, and for something really simple like this, it is overkill. But classes get complicated fast, and it ends up there's a good reason for it: static.

If a method or property is static, it means that it belongs to the class instead of the object. Let's say this is our code:

```
static var emailAddress:String;
```

To get at this property, you'd write:

```
CustomerInfo.emailAddress
```

Static properties belong to the class, not to any of the objects.

For example, the Math class has only static properties. You'll never see

```
var myMath:Object = new Math();
```

Nope. Not once.

You will see

```
Math.PI
```

In this case, PI is a property of the Math class. It's a static property.

You can even check the Math.as file in the Classes directory, which contains the line

```
static var PI:Number;
```

There's a lot more than can be done with classes, but that's beyond the scope of this book.

Don't forget to save your work as a separate file and call it CustomerInfo.as. This part is vital. Otherwise, Flash won't recognize it as a class and will ignore it, and your code won't do a darn thing.

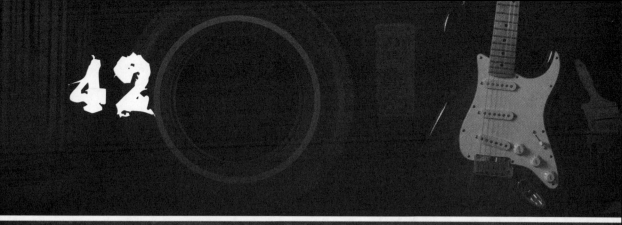

42

Extending the Movie Clip Class

 o start with, we should talk about classes and subclasses.

Classes and Subclasses

In OOP, you can create classes that borrow the properties and methods from other classes. For example, if the class SuperHero has a fly() method, you could create a SideKick class that borrows from the SuperHero class, and the SideKick class would then be able to fly() as well.

When we allow one class to use another's properties and methods, it is called creating a subclass. The SideKick class becomes a subclass of SuperHero.

Arr, ye syntax be:

```
class SideKick extends Superhero
{
    // SideKick-specific stuff
}
```

Code Fix!

```
class Fall extends MovieClip {

    // constructor
    function Fall(mc:MovieClip){
    }

    function moveUp(){
        _y -= 1;
    }

    function moveDown(){
        _y += 20;
    }
}
```

Be sure to call this `Fall.as`.

See how we get to use _y? We didn't set that property in our class—we didn't have to. It magically appeared because we get everything that the `MovieClip` class gives its object (that would be movie clips).

This passing of methods and properties is known as *inheritance*. In a sense, `Fall` is a child of `MovieClip` and thus inherits all of its properties and methods.

Okay, this may make sense from a conceptual standpoint, but you probably won't really understand it until we actually apply it: Make a symbol of anything and call it `Ball`. In its Linkage menu, make sure its class is `Fall`, as in Figure 42.1.

That's how we connect a movie clip with a class.

```
this.attachMovie("Ball", "ball1",1);

ball1.onEnterFrame = function()
{
    ball1.moveDown();
}
```

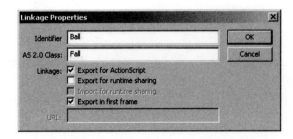

Figure 42.1

Linkage Menu

See what's happening? We have a regular movie clip, `ball`, but it's got a new method called `moveDown()` that no one movie clip has. This can be particularly useful if you want a bunch of movie clips to have access to a certain method or property.

43

Adding Methods to Built-in Classes

already mentioned that AS2 is compiled into AS1. Thus, we shouldn't be too surprised to hear that AS1 code works fine in MX2004. In order to add methods to built-in classes like Array, Strong, Math, and XML, we have to dive into AS1 code and use something called a *prototype*.

arrayShuffle.as

```
Array.prototype.distinctShuffle = function () {

    trace("in distinct shuffle");
    result = [];
    for (posArray = [], i = 0; i < this.length; posArray[i] = i++) {}
    for (last = this.length - 1; last >= 0; last--)
    {
        selected = this[last];
        rand = random(posArray.length - 1);
        lastPos = posArray.getPos(last);
        if (lastPos == null)
        {
```

```
                        result[posArray[rand]] = selected;
                        posArray.splice(rand, 1);
                }
                else
                {
                        posArray.splice(lastPos, 1);
                        result[posArray[rand]] = selected;
                        posArray.splice(rand, 1);
                        posArray.push(last);
                }
        }
        return result;
}


Array.prototype.getPos = function (item) {
        for (i = 0; i < this.length; ++i) {
                if (this[i] == item) {
                        return i;
                }
        }
        return null;
}
```

What we've done is add a method to the **Array** class, which is something you can't do in AS2. It's a little strange using older code to do something the new code can't do. MX2004 feels a little like a transition product, using AS2 but not leaving AS1 completely behind yet.

What Is This Prototype Thing?

A prototype is something that exists in AS1 only—it isn't AS2 code. The fact that you can use "prototype" reveals that AS1 doesn't use a formal class structure like AS2 or Java or similar languages. AS1 has what's called prototype-based inheritance. Here's how it works: Classes are defined by top-level objects. These objects are **Math**, **Array**, **String**, and the like. Each object has a property called **prototype**. When an instance of a class is created, like an array or string, it inherits all of the methods and properties that live in the prototype of the top-level object.

For example, if you add a method to the **Array** class's prototype, then all other arrays would also have that new method. That's what we did up above.

So let's actually use this code.

Move Code

```
// Don't use import - that's for classes, and this isn't a class
#include "arrayShuffle.as"

a = ["a", "b", "c", "d", "e", "f", "g", "h", "i", "j"];
b = a.distinctShuffle();

trace("original array : " + a);
trace("shuffled array : " + b);
```

Run it:

```
in distinct shuffle
original array : a,b,c,d,e,f,g,h,i,j
shuffled array : g,h,e,a,b,d,j,i,c,f
```

PART XII
Events and Listeners

Events, Handlers, and Listeners
on() and onClipEvent()
Event Methods
MovieClipLoader
addListener()
addEventListener()

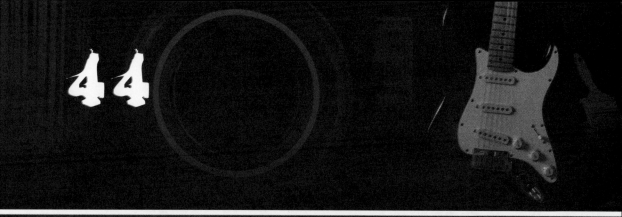

44

Events, Handlers, and Listeners

Knowing how events, event handlers, and listeners work is vital if you hope to code any real interaction in your Flash movie. So, harken well.

Events are actions that occur while a Flash movie is playing. For example,

DO OR DIE:

> > Stuff happens. Your code reacts.

- The playhead enters a frame.
- The user presses the mouse button.
- Some XML finishes loading.

So, an event is a pretty broad thing. There are two kinds: user events and system events.

A user event is an action the user performs:

- Hits a key
- Presses the mouse button
- Moves the mouse
- Types in a text field

A system event is an action that Flash performs:

- Loads a movie
- Retrieves some variables
- Enters the playhead into a frame

Broadcasters

Broadcasters are the things that the events happen to. Broadcasters can be

- A `Mouse` object
- A `Key` object
- A `MovieClip` object
- A `Stage` object
- A `LoadVars` object
- An `XML` object
- Pretty much any object, when you get down to it

For example, when the user clicks the mouse button, the `Mouse` object sees this and hollers out at the rest of the Flash movie, "AAAGH! CLICK!! AAAGH!" This is broadcasting. The `Mouse` object then relaxes until someone does it again.
Here is how to handle events:

- Handling an event means doing something in response to an event.
- Use this simple mnemonic device: "An event happened! Holy cow! How am I going to handle it?!" Saying this loudly while programming will cause it to stick in your mind and in the minds of those around you. Practice often. It's helpful. Really.

So, an event handler is a chunk of code that runs when a certain event occurs. Types of event handlers include

- Event handler methods
- Event listeners
- Button and movie clip event handlers

Event Handler Methods

Event handler methods look like this:

```
myButton.onPress = function()
{
    // do something
}
```

Or, if you want to get a little fancy, like this:

```
myButton.onPress = jumpUpAndDown;

function jumpUpAndDown()
{
    // jump
}
```

Note that

```
myButton.onPress = jumpUpAndDown();
```

is wrong. No parentheses are required in this situation.

Why code your event handler this way?

Sometimes it's easier to do it this way than to create that whole event listener (see below). You can also assign multiple events to the same handler as so:

```
myButton.onPress = jumpUpAndDown;
yourButton.onPress = jumpUpAndDown;

function jumpUpAndDown() {
    // jump
}
```

However, if you're using components, you're stuck with listeners. Read on.

Listeners

A listener is an object, just a plain ol' object.

```
var myListener:Object = new Object();
```

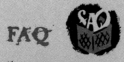

FAQ

Tom Asks Why

Why would you ever use an event listener?
Because sometimes it's helpful for a bunch of objects pointing at the same function:

```
listener = new Object();
listener.click = function(evtObj){
  trace("The " + evtObj.target.label + " button was clicked");
}
myButton.addEventListener("click", listener);
yourButton.addEventListener("click", listener);
thatGuysButton.addEventListener("click", listener);
```

You could conceivably have two listeners for a single event:

```
listener1 = new Object();
listener2 = new Object();

listener1.click = function(evtObj){
  trace("The " + evtObj.target.label + " button was clicked");
}
listener2.click = function(evtObj){
  trace("Me too!");
}

myButton.addEventListener("click", listener1);
myButton.addEventListener("click", listener2);
```

In general, addEventListener is really meant for components.

You've created an object that is ready to be a listener. How does it work? Say you have a button component (that's a component button, not a regular button, mind you) called myButton.

```
listener = new Object();
listener.click = function(evtObj)
{
  trace("The " + evtObj.target.label + " button was clicked");
}
myButton.addEventListener("click", listener);
```

The order may seem backwards, but this is the way to do it.

What's That evtObj Thing?

When an event occurs, not only the fact of the event broadcast (the "AAAGH! CLICK!! AAAGH!"), but also information about the event—where on the Stage it happened, what it happened to, and so on—is placed in a little object called the **event** object. This object is passed to any function handling the event. In this case, that's evtObj.

Notice we use addEventListener() here. That's what you use when you add a listener to a component. See more in Topic 49, addEventListener.

Movie Clips and Buttons

You can use the old and busted way of handling events on buttons and movie clips, like the following:

```
// for a button
on(press)
{
    play();
}
```

or

```
// for a movie clip
onClipEvent(enterFrame)
{
    // do stuff
}
```

I prefer to use event methods (new hotness). That is,

```
myButton.onPress = function()
{
    // do stuff
}
```

It's a cleaner way to organize your code, IMHO.

on() and onClipEvent()

his is code you'd place directly on movie clip instances or buttons (which I don't recommend doing, in general). The code doesn't go on frames, but on the objects themselves.

I recently had to create a little tutorial for a Charles Schwab intranet that had to work in Flash 5 and above, so it can happen.

on()

on() is used only for buttons. For a component button, use this syntax:

```
on(click)
{
    trace("May I help you?");
}
```

Components are a world unto themselves, which is why they have different events than normal movie clips have.

For a regular, noncomponent button, use this syntax:

```
on(press)
{
    trace("Wait! I wasn't ready.");
}
```

onClipEvent()

onClipEvent() is used only for movie clips. The syntax is exactly as above. Here are the events you can use:

- load
- unload
- enterFrame (This is the one I most often use. It's called once for every frame in your movie. It allows you to do repetitive code that builds on itself, without having to write any looping.)
- mouseMove
- mouseDown
- mouseUp
- keyDown
- keyUp
- data

46

Event Methods

DO OR DIE:

➢ ➢ Event methods designate a certain function to run when a certain event occurs.

➢ ➢ Event methods are also called callback functions.

vent methods are pretty simple. Are you ready?

You. The kid with the ponytail in Oakland. You're not ready. We're waiting.

Fine. Good. Thank you—and get a haircut. Ponytails are so 1996.

Code Fix!

```
submit_btn.onPress = function()
{
    // do something
}
```

What? That's it? That's easy! Yup.
Here's a mild variation:

```
submit_btn.onPress = jumpUpAndDown;

Function jumpUpAndDown(evtObj)
{
    // do stuff
}
```

Also easy, right? Darn straight. Pointing to a separate function can be useful if more than one component in your movie can use the same function.

```
bird_mc.onPress = swingBackAndForth;
fish_mc.onPress = swingBackAndForth;
dinosaur_mc.onPress = swingBackAndForth;

function swingBackAndForth(evtObj)
{
    // brilliant code
}
```

Note that even though you're referring to a function, don't use parentheses. That is,

```
bird_mc.onPress = swingBackAndForth();
```

is wrong. Make sure you do it like this:

```
bird_mc.onPress = swingBackAndForth;
```

MovieClipLoader

f you want to carefully and exactly follow the progress of a loading movie clip, then you'll like MovieClipLoader. Otherwise, you'll be fine sticking with loadMovie().

MovieClipLoader is useful because of its events. Once a movie clip starts loading, you have access to the following:

- onLoadStart (triggered when first bytes are downloaded; good for images)

- onLoadInit (triggered when first frames are downloaded; good for movie clips)

- onLoadProgress (triggered while loading happens)

- onLoadCompleted (triggered when movie or image is finished loading)

- onLoadError (triggered if the move failed to load completely)

Note that you get to use these events only if you're loading the movie using

```
loader = new MovieClipLoader();
loader.loadClip("yourMovie.swf", this);
```

Syntax for loadClip() is

```
movieClipLoaderInstance.loadClip(url, target);
```

If you load a movie using MovieClipLoader, you also get to use a method called getProgress():

```
progressObj = loader.getProgress("yourMovie.swf");
trace(progressObj.bytesLoaded + " of " + progressObj.bytesTotal);
```

addListener()

ddListener() is a method you can use when you want to latch a listener onto certain objects. These objects are as follows:

- Key
- Stage
- MovieClipLoader
- Selection
- TextField
- Mouse

This won't make any sense until you see the code.

DO OR DIE:

> > Create an object whose purpose in life is to monitor something, like the mouse, and see if any event happens to it.

> > Only certain objects can have addListener() used on them.

Code Fix!

```
keyboardListener = new Object();
keyboardListener.onKeyDown = function ()
{
    trace("You squashed a key.");
}
```

```
keyboardListener.onKeyUp = function ()
{
    trace("You released a key. ");
}


Key.addListener(keyBoardListener);
```

What the Sam Hill?

See what's going on? We create an empty object and set it up as a listener for the Key object, which continually scans the keyboard to see if the user is banging on it.

When we use **addListener()**, that listener object (**keyboardListener** in this case) is looking for any event that happens on the keyboard.

Events

Here's a list of all the objects and events you can use **addListener()** with:

- Key.onKeyUp
- Key.onKeyDown
- Stage.onResize
- MovieClipLoader.onLoadComplete
- MovieClipLoader.onLoadError
- MovieClipLoader.onLoadInit
- MovieClipLoader.onLoadProgress
- MovieClipLoader.onLoadStart
- Selection.onSetFocus
- TextField.onChanged
- TextField.onScroller

removeListener()

If you want to stop hearing from the keyboard or mouse or other device, you can remove the listener:

```
Key.removeListener(keyboardListener);
```

addEventListener()

 ou read earlier about **addListener()**, which is the way to add a listener object to

- Mouse
- Key
- MovieClipLoader
- Selection
- Stage
- TextField

DO OR DIE:

> > addEventListener is the only way to add a listener object to a component.

> > It can listen only for a specific event (hence the name).

Now we're looking at **addEventListener** (notice racy "Event" in the middle there). **AddEventListener** is meant only for components, like checkboxes and radio buttons and such. It can listen only for a certain event. Other than that, it's just like **addListener()**.

Enough of your yammering, boy. Where's my. . .

Code Fix!

```
buttonListener = new Object();
buttonListener.click = function (evtObj)
{
    trace("The " + evtObj.target.label + " button was clicked. ");
}
submit1_btn.addEventListener("click", buttonListener);
submit2_btn.addEventListener("click", buttonListener);
```

What the Sam Hill?

First, we create your basic empty object.

```
submit1_btn.addEventListener("click", buttonListener);
```

Then, we tell the object what to do.

```
buttonListener.click = function (evtObj)
{
    trace("The " + evtObj.target.label + " button was clicked. ");
}
```

Wait a minute. We all know the event for pressing a button is **onPress**, not **click**, right? Well, this is a component button, not a regular one, and component buttons have different events than normal buttons have. This means that when you're using **addEventListener** on your components, you'd better make sure you're using component-friendly events.

Don't forget the **.click** part of the event handler.

The **evtObj** parameter is the **event** object, which is created every time an event occurs. The **event** object contains information about where the event happened and what it happened to (**target**, in this case). This can be useful if you need to decide which button (or checkbox or menu item or whatever) was clicked.

Next, we attach the listener to a couple of buttons.

```
submit1_btn.addEventListener("click", buttonListener);
submit2_btn.addEventListener("click", buttonListener);
```

This is one thing about listener objects that's handy—you can use them on a number of different components.

Don't forget that you can remove a listener object with the **removeListener()** method:

```
submit1_btn.removeListener(buttonListener);
```

PART. XIII

Some New UI Components

DataGrid Component

This component is kinda cool. It's essentially a table with rows, columns, cells, and such. Imagine an HTML `<table>` you can populate dynamically (well, you can do that with DHMTL, but using the DataGrid component is easier) and that users can edit the text in the table cells.

Programmatically, you can add columns and rows on the fly. You can also programmatically edit the cells—that is, change their value at runtime. This functionality is useful for a dynamic-report-generation tool (marketing folk tend to love reports, and if you can create a nice system for them, they'll like you).

Let's get going!

DO OR DIE:

> > Using the DataGrid component is a nice way to dynamically build a table in Flash.

Code Fix!

Create a new movie. Drag a DataGrid component onto the Stage and call it `test_grid`, as in Figure 50.1.

On the first frame, add the following:

```
people = new Array(
    {Name:"Annie", Job:"Pirate"},
    {Name:"Misha", Job:"Monster Robot"},
    {Name:"Zach", Job:"Drooler"},
    {Name:"Achilles", Job:"Cobbler"}
```

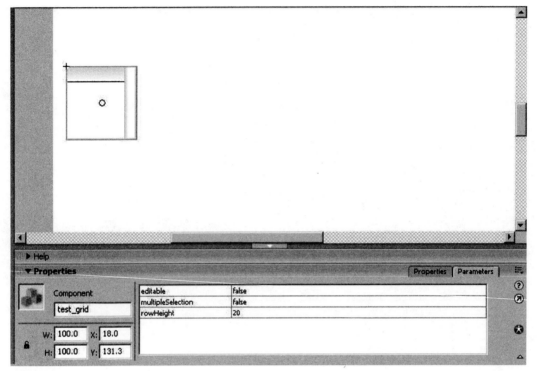

Figure 50.1

test_grid

```
);
test_grid.dataProvider = people;
test_grid.setSize(300,200);
test_grid.editable = true;
```

Test the movie, and revealed to you is the table in Figure 50.2.

If you click on the table cells, you can change them right in the Flash movie, as in Figure 50.3.

What the Sam Hill?

You probably understand what the `setSize()` method and `editable` property do. The whole `array` and `dataProvider` thing may be a little fuzzy, though.

`people` is an array of four objects. Each of those four objects has two properties: `Name` and `Job`. Notice that to tell ActionScript you're creating an object, you need to use the curly braces. For example,

```
myObject = { property1: value1, property2: value2 };
```

As it happens, DataGrids like objects. It uses the property name as the column header and the value as the table cell value.

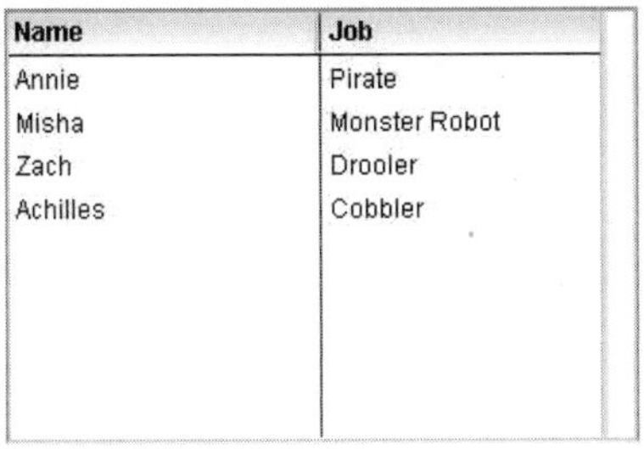

Figure 50.2

The Populated DataGrid

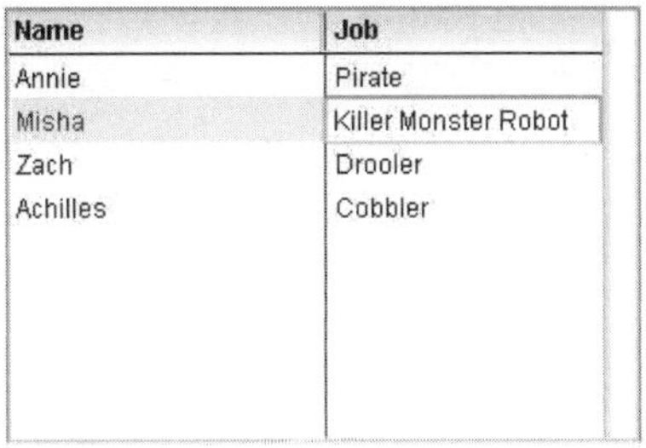

Figure 50.3

Editing DataGrid Cells

The names of the columns are set by the properties of the first object. For example, try this code out:

```
people = new Array(
    {Name:"Annie",    Jab:"Pirate"},
    {Nome:"Misha",    Job:"Monster Robot"},
    {Name:"Zach",     Job:"Drooler"},
    {Name:"Achilles", Jab:"Cobbler"}
);
```

I bolded what's been changed. Test the movie and you get Figure 50.4.

So, that's your introduction. Let's get fancier.

First, add three buttons to the Flash movie, as in Figure 50.5.

Call them

- `hair_btn`
- `bigplans_btn`
- `single_btn`

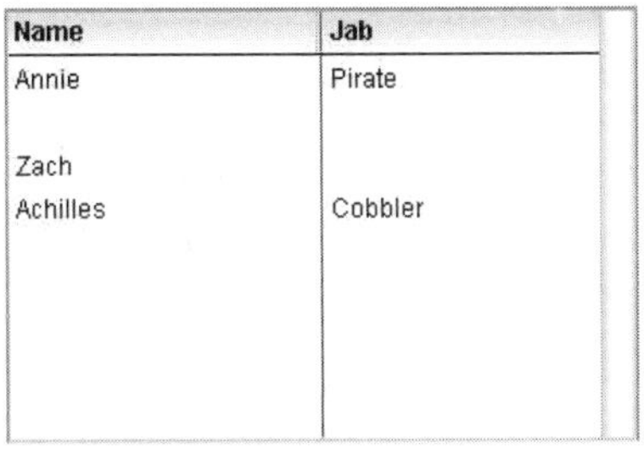

Figure 50.4

The Tweaked DataGrid

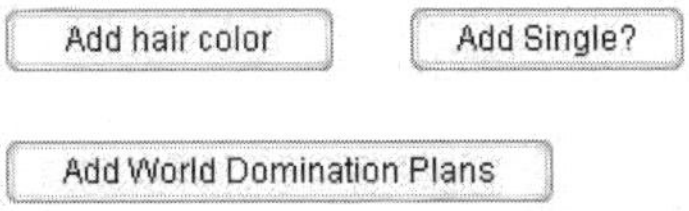

Figure 50.5

DataGrid Buttons

Our plan is that clicking those buttons will add and remove columns from out data grid. Click a button to add the column, then click again to remove it.

Code Fix!

Add the following below the existing code:

```
var gridHeight:Number = 200;

function toggleColumn(columnName, buttonName)
{
    var foundColumn:Boolean = false;

    // find the column
    for (i=0; i<test_grid.columnNames.length; i++)
    {
        if (test_grid.columnNames[i] == columnName)
        {
            foundColumn = true;

            test_grid.removeColumnAt(i);
            test_grid.setSize(test_grid.width-175,gridHeight);
            test_grid.spaceColumnsEqually();
            _root[buttonName].label = "Add " + columnName;
        }
    }
    if(!foundColumn)
    {
        test_grid.setSize(test_grid.width+175,gridHeight);
        test_grid.addColumn(columnName);
        test_grid.spaceColumnsEqually();
        _root[buttonName].label = "Remove " + columnName;
    }
}

hair_btn.onRelease = function ()
{
    toggleColumn("Hair Color", this._name);
}

bigplans_btn.onRelease = function ()
{
    toggleColumn("World Domination", this._name);
}
```

```
single_btn.onRelease = function ()
{
    toggleColumn("Single?", this._name);
}
```

What the Sam Hill?

What we've done is pass a column name and a button name to the function.
That's it. Two names. Not what they are supposed to do—just two names.

The function decides what to do based on what's there. If there's a column, it
removes it. If there is no column, it adds one. Then it changes the button name.

```
// find the column
for (i=0; i<test_grid.columnNames.length; i++)
{
    if (test_grid.columnNames[i] == columnName)
    {
        foundColumn = true;

        test_grid.removeColumnAt(i);
        test_grid.setSize(test_grid.width-175,gridHeight);
        test_grid.spaceColumnsEqually();
        _root[buttonName].label = "Add " + columnName;
    }
}
```

We loop over the `columnNames array` and check out if the DataGrid's column
name is the same that the function was given. If the column already exists, that
means we're trying to remove it, and fortunately, there's an easy method called
`removeColumnAt()` that does the job. However, this doesn't resize the component—you just end up with a big space where the column used to be, as in
Figure 50.6.

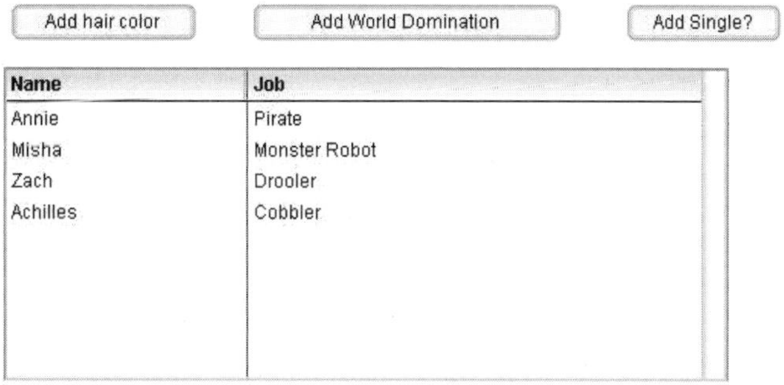

Figure 50.6

*Simply
Removing the
Column*

That's why we have to reset the component size. We then space the columns out nicely, using the very handy `spaceColumnsEqually()` method (users can also alter the column width themselves, though).

Finally, we change the button label.

That's how to remove a column. To add a column, do this:

```
if(!foundColumn)
{
    test_grid.setSize(test_grid.width+175,gridHeight);
    test_grid.addColumn(columnName);
    test_grid.spaceColumnsEqually();
    _root[buttonName].label = "Remove " + columnName;
}
```

You can tell what's going on here. We make the component bigger, add a column, space everything out, and change the button text.

FAQ

Tom Asks Why

Probably the most obvious application of the DataGrid component is to display record sets from a database, but you could read in data from an XML file as well.

Label Component

There isn't a whole heck of a lot going on with the Label component. It's essentially a stripped-down text field. It doesn't do anything except display text. You can have HTML in it, but that's about it.

Like other components, Label has an initial set size. To see this, fire up a new Flash movie, drag a Label onto it, call it **name_label**, and enter this code:

```
name_label.text = "Here is a longer label than this component is
  initially ready for.";
```

Test your movie, and you get Figure 51.1.

Eh. Notice that we used **name_label.text**, not **name_label.label** as you might expect.

```
name_label.text = "Here is a longer label than this component is
  initially ready for.";
name_label.autoSize = true;
```

This solves the truncation problem (Figure 51.2).

yawn

Here is a longer l:

Figure 51.1

Truncated Text

Figure 51.2

All Da Text

> Here is a longer label than this component is initially ready for.

All right, let's bring this boring topic to a rapid close. To use HTML in your label, you use this line:

```
name_label.html = true;
name_label.text = "Here is a <b>longer label</b> than this
  component is initially ready for.";
name_label.autoSize = true;
```

Note that you can't use **
** to force line breaks.

Styles

You can use style with Labels, as well.

```
name_label.fontStyle = "italic";
name_label.text = "Here is a longer label than this component is
  initially ready for.";
name_label.autoSize = true;
```

This results in a full line of italicized text. However, a Label can't use HMTL and styles at the same time. For example, this

```
name_label.fontStyle = "italic";
name_label.html = true;
name_label.text = "Here is a <b>longer label</b> than this
  component is initially ready for.";
name_label.autoSize = true;
```

would have zero italics in it.

Here are all the styles you can use (they probably look familiar):

- color
- embedFonts
- fontFamily
- fontStyle
- fontWeight
- textAlign
- textDecoration

yawn
Nap time.

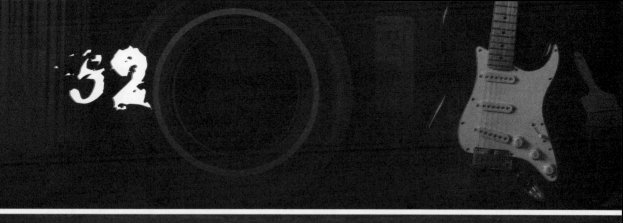

Loader

The Loader component is used to load JPEGs and SWFs into your movie. Flash already has a couple of other ways to do this, but, well, here's another one.

DO OR DIE:

>> The Loader component's purpose in life is to load external content such as a JPEG or SWF.

Code Fix!

Open up a new movie, drag in a Loader component, and call it `img_loader`.

```
img_loader.load("cube.jpg");

loaderListener = new Object();
loaderListener.complete = function(eventObject)
{
        // this is fired even when it's something unloadable,
        // like a GIF
        trace(img_loader.content);
        trace(img_loader.contentPath);
}
img_loader.addEventListener("complete", loaderListener);
```

You've seen listeners and events already, so I won't go over them again. Figure 52.1 shows you what the movie looks like.

Figure 52.1

It's Loaded

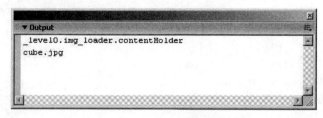

Sometimes, you may want to deal with content that's in a component instead of in a movie clip. For example, you can now move your little cube by moving the loader component:

```
img_loader.move(0,0);
```

The Loader component is good for doing something while your movie or giant JPEG is loading:

- `Loader.bytesLoaded`
- `Loader.bytesTotal`
- `Loader.percentLoaded`
- `Loader.progress`
- `Loader.complete`

Numeric Stepper

The Numeric Stepper is the little bugger shown in Figure 53.1. Click the up and down arrows to change the value.

Neato.

The Stepper is only good for letting the user choose a number quickly. Thus, you'd better be able to get to that value. Here's how:

- Open a new movie.
- Drag in a stepper and a button.
- Call the stepper numBeers_Step and the button step_btn.
- Type yon code in the first frame:

```
numBeers_step.setSize(50, 20);
step_btn.onRelease = function()
{
    trace(numBeers_step.value);
}
```

Test the movie, and you get Figure 53.2.

DO OR DIE:

> > There is not much to Numeric Stepper. Numbers go up. Numbers go down. Numbers go up. Numbers go down.

Figure 53.1

Numeric Stepper

Figure 53.2

Getting the Value from a Numeric Stepper

If you don't do anything to it, the Numeric Stepper holds values from 0 to 10. You'll want to set your own minimum and maximum values, and maybe even a little step size. Here's how to do it:

```
numBeers_step.stepSize = 1.02;
numBeers_step.minimum = -20;
numBeers_step.maximum = 24;

// otherwise, it'll start at zero
numBeers_step.value = -20;
```

You can also react every time the user clicks on one of the arrows:

```
stepListener = new Object();
stepListener.change = function(evt)
{
    trace("stomp");
}
myStepper.addEventListener("change", stepListener);
```

Hit the up arrow a few times, and you've got Figure 53.3. Like I said, there is not much to this one.

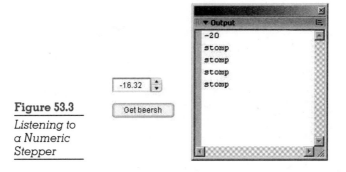

Figure 53.3

Listening to a Numeric Stepper

Tree

igure 54.1 shows what a properly filled Tree component looks like.

Tree is a way to traverse XML data. That's all it's
really for. This can be XML that you load from somewhere
else, or it can be an XML object that you built internally in
Flash.

▼ 📂 classes
   ▼ 📂 XML for Dogs
      📄 Full
   ▶ 📁 Tango Fundamentals
   ▼ 📂 Black Rock City Civics
      📄 20,000 spots left

Figure 54.1

*Tree Component
with Data*

Code Fix!

Open a new movie. Drag that Tree component to the Stage, and call it **stage_tree**. Make it 600 pixels wide and 300 pixels high.

In your text editor of choice, create **classes.xml**:

```
<classes>
    <class>
            <title>XML for Dogs</title>
            <availability>Full</availability>
    </class>
    <class>
            <title>Tango Fundamentals</title>
            <availability>3 spots left</availability>
    </class>
    <class>
            <title>Black Rock City Civics</title>
            <availability>20,000 spots left</availability>
    </class>
</classes>
```

Here's your ActionScript code:

```
var classes_xml:XML = new XML();
// the ignoreWhite thing is really important
classes_xml.ignoreWhite = true;
classes_xml.load("classes.xml");
classes_xml.onLoad = function()
{
    classes_tree.dataProvider = classes_xml;
}
```

Test the movie. Surprise! It looks like Figure 54.2.

Holy messy type Function, Batman! What the heck is this?

It turns out that Tree does something darned annoying: It needs the XML to be in a very specific format in order to display it properly. It isn't designed to take just any XML document and spit it out.

All right. So what's this Tree-friendly XML? Well, it goes a little something like this:

```
<node label="classes">
    <node label="XML for Dogs">
            <node label="Full" />
    </node>
```

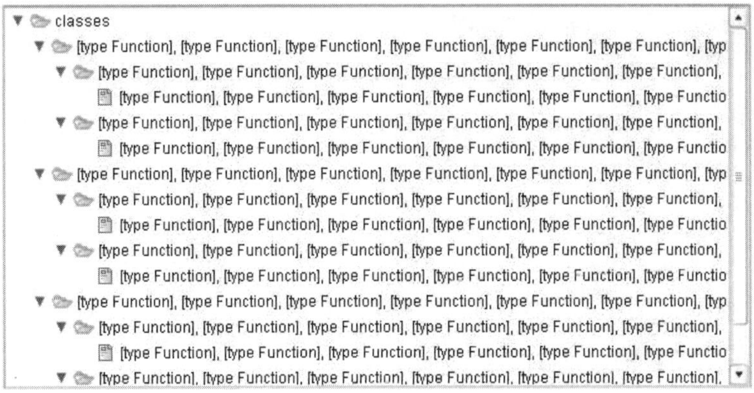

Figure 54.2

A Mess

```
<node label="Tango Fundamentals">
        <node label="3 spots left" />
</node>
<node label="Black Rock City Civics">
        <node label="20,000 spots left" />
</node>
</node>
```

Pretty simple stuff. Flash decides to display a little folder icon or a little document icon based on whether or not there are any child nodes (which makes sense).

You can set your own icon using the `Tree.setIcon()` method.

> **<side>**
> If you think about it, that makes sense, though—XML is so flexible, it'd be pretty difficult to come up with a component that handled all XML gracefully.
> **</side>**

```
classes_xml.onLoad = function()
{
    classes_tree.dataProvider = classes_xml;
    classes_tree.setIcon(classes_tree.getTreeNodeAt(0), "closed",
      "open");
}
```

What the Sam Hill?

After we set the `dataProvider`, we tell `classes_tree` that the first node's icons are found in the Library. The icon for a closed node is the symbol with the `closed` identifier, and the icon for an open node is the symbol with the `open` identifier.

Figure 54.3 shows the super-simple closed image (note the registration mark in the upper left—that's where you want it) and the Linkage dialog box where I call it "closed."

Figure 54.3

*The closed
Symbol*

Populating the Tree
with an Internal XML Document

Just because we can (and this is the most likely way you'll populate this component), let's use an internal XML document to populate the Tree.

```
var classes_xml:XML = new XML();

// create XML elements
classes_node = classes_xml.createElement("node");
dogs_node = classes_node.cloneNode(true);
full_node = classes_node.cloneNode(true);
tango_node = classes_node.cloneNode(true);
three_node = classes_node.cloneNode(true);
burn_node = classes_node.cloneNode(true);
twenty_node = classes_node.cloneNode(true);

// add attributes
classes_node.attributes.label = "Classes";
dogs_node.attributes.label = "XML For Dogs";
full_node.attributes.label = "Full";
tango_node.attributes.label = "Tango Fundamentals";
three_node.attributes.label = "3 spots left";
burn_node.attributes.label = "Black Rock City Civics";
twenty_node.attributes.label = "20,000 spots left";

// place elements
classes_xml.appendChild(classes_node);
```

```
classes_node.appendChild(dogs_node);
classes_node.appendChild(tango_node);
classes_node.appendChild(burn_node);

dogs_node.appendChild(full_node);
tango_node.appendChild(three_node);
burn_node.appendChild(twenty_node);

// fill the tree
classes_tree.dataProvider = classes_xml;
```

> **FYI**
> The Tree component is composed of two sets of APIs: the Tree class and the TreeDataProvider interface.

Test it out—it's the same result as when we used the loaded file.

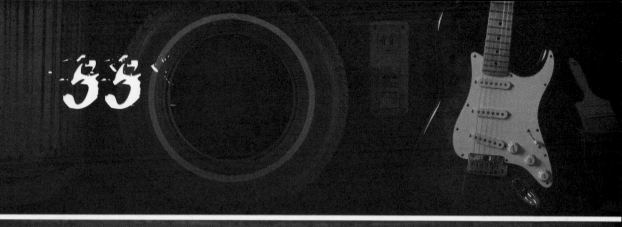

Window Component

The Window component works fine. However, the API you have to wade through to get it to work is less, uh, streamlined than some of the other components. That is, it's a pain in the lambada to code.

Figure 55.1 shows you what the window looks like.

To create a window, fire up a new movie. Drag a Window component to the Stage and delete it (it has to be in the Library). Then, in the first frame, bang on your keyboard until you have the following:

```
import mx.managers.PopUpManager;
import mx.containers.Window;

var loginWindow = PopUpManager.createPopUp(_root, Window, true);
loginWindow.setSize(240,210);
loginWindow.title = "Change Password";
```

Yes, this is different syntax from any other UI component. *shrug* It's clunky, but so be it. Let's hope Flash MX 2005 Professional Let's Put More Words In the Name of the Product has a cleaner way to do Windows.

Figure 55.2 shows you what the above code results in.

DO OR DIE:

> > The Window component opens up a little window and sticks a movie clip in it.

> > It does not have the most intuitive API, though.

Figure 55.1
A Window with a Movie Clip in It

Change Password	
Password	
Confirm Password	
	OK

Figure 55.2

Bare-Bones Window

Now, you'll want two things here:

1. You'll want your Window to contain something.
2. You'll want your Window to appear only at certain times.

Let's slap something in that window. Something simple, like the stuff in Figure 55.3.

Our movie clip is very simple: two text fields, two TextInput components, and a Button component. Check out what happens in the Linkage box, though:

in the AS 2.0 Class box → mx.core.View

I did this because the documentation told me to (and it makes sense, since the `Window` class inherits from `ScrollView`, which inherits from `View`). But it isn't necessary. You can leave the ActionScript 2.0 Class box totally blank and get the exact same effect.

Surprising? Why, yes! Shocking! A potential omission in technical documentation?! Horrors!

So, now we're over that—let's add a button that pops the window up, since you probably don't want your movie/interface/thing to start with the window floating above everything.

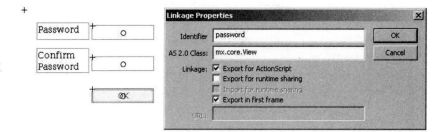

Figure 55.3

A Wee Movie Clip

Pop-Up Window

Add a button called **password_btn** to your movie.

```
// Pop-up Window
import mx.managers.PopUpManager;
import mx.containers.Window;

var buttonListener:Object = new Object();
buttonListener.click = function()
{
```

```
    var loginWindow = PopUpManager.createPopUp(_root, Window, true);
    loginWindow.setSize(240,210);
    loginWindow.title = "Change Password";
    loginWindow.contentPath = "password";
}


password_btn.addEventListener("click", buttonListener);
```

It's pretty similar to what you've seen before, what with the events and listeners and all. You're smart. You get it.

Close the Window

Now that we've created a window and put something in it, we'll probably want to close it at some point. One way to do this is the following:

```
buttonListener.click = function()
{
    var loginWindow = PopUpManager.createPopUp(_root, Window, true);
    loginWindow.setSize(240,210);
    loginWindow.title = "Change Password";
    loginWindow.contentPath = "password";

    // close button
    loginWindow.closeButton = true;
}
```

See the code in bold? It results in Figure 55.4.

Try it. Click on it. What happens?

Not a darn thing. Nothing closes. The reasoning behind this, I hear, is that you the developer might want many different things to happen when a user clicks the close button. Thus, Macromedia decided not to give this little guy any default behavior but to leave its behavior up to you.

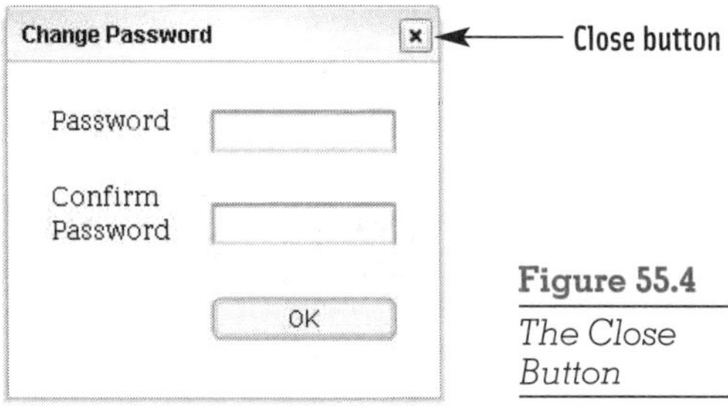

Figure 55.4

The Close
Button

Suppose you want this close button to, say, close the window:

```
buttonListener.click = function()
{
    // create the window
    var loginWindow = PopUpManager.createPopUp(_root, Window, true);
    loginWindow.setSize(240,210);
    loginWindow.title = "Change Password";
    loginWindow.contentPath = "password";

    // close button code
    // this has to be in the click event handler,
    // or it doesn't work
    loginWindow.closeButton = true;
    var closeWindowListener:Object = new Object();
    closeWindowListener.click = function(evtObj)
    {
        loginWindow.deletePopUp();
    }
    loginWindow.addEventListener("click", closeWindowListener);
}
```

The code in bold is the stuff you care about. It's a simple listener/event model you've seen a dozen times before. Read the comments—they're true. This code has to live in the buttonListener event handler, or it doesn't work—pressing the close button has no effect.

Also notice, of course, the deletePopUp() method, which closes the window.

Another Way to Close

```
buttonListener.click = function()
{
    // create the window
    var loginWindow = PopUpManager.createPopUp(_root, Window, true);
    loginWindow.setSize(240,210);
    loginWindow.title = "Change Password";
    loginWindow.contentPath = "password";
    loginWindow.closeButton = true;

    loginWindow.addEventListener("click", {click: function(evtObj)
        {evtObj.target.deletePopUp();}});
}
```

This code is more succinct, but it's harder to read, and I like my code to be readable.

Loading a JPEG to the Window

```
myWindow.contentPath = "cube.jpg";
```

This line works just fine. Note that's content*Path*, not content.

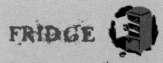
Issues

The Window component is well known for having issues, and one of the outstanding issues seems to be `Window.content`, by which you, ideally, can alter the content of what's in the Window via ActionScript, like so:

```
m = myWindow.content;
m.password_txt.text = "homer";
```

I couldn't get it to work. Anyone else have any luck?

Supposedly, the **content** is like the **_root** of the movie clip that's inside the window.

> **Note**
>
> You can also create a window with this syntax:
>
> `PopUpManager.createPopUp(`*parentMovieClip*`, Window, `*modality*`, `*initObj*`, `*broadcastOutsideEvents*`)`
>
> `modality` and `broadcastOutsideEvents` are both Booleans (only true or false values). Modality means the window is on top of everything else in your movie (you'll usually want this to be true), and everything else is disabled except for the window.
>
> Modality is simulated by creating a large, transparent window underneath the Window component. Due to the way transparent windows are rendered, you may notice a slight dimming of the objects under the transparent window. The effective transparency can be set by changing the `_global.style.modalTransparency` value from 0 (fully transparent) to 100 (opaque). If you make the window partially transparent, you can also set the color of the window by changing the Modal skin in the default theme.

PART XIV

Data Binding

Yes, Data Binding

36

Yes, Data Binding

No, Really--What's Data Binding?

Data binding is creating a connection between something on the Stage, like a text field, a button, a counter, or just about anything, and a variable or some other bit of data. The two are bound to each other. When the data changes, the thing on the Stage changes automatically.

Assigning a variable to a text field is like a poor man's data binding.

You can also bind two text fields to each other. One of them will act as a source field, the other as the destination.

That's how binding works—there's always a source and a destination. The information flows in only one direction. It never goes from destination to source.

You'd Better Do This First

In order to create data binding at runtime (that is, to do it with ActionScript), you must have the DataBindingClasses component in your Library. Here's how to put it there:

```
Window → Other Panels → Common Libraries → Classes
```

Tom Asks Why

Why bother with data binding? Because it makes your life easier. Instead of explicitly updating your little doo-dad on the Stage, just bind it to the variable, and you can stop thinking about it—it'll update on its own.

Choose DataBindingClasses. Drag it to the stage, and delete it. Voila! It's in your Library.

Code Fix!

About time! Imagine two text fields name **src_txt** and **dest_txt**. When the user (or ActionScript) places something into **src_txt** and then moves focus to something else, the text in **dest_txt** is automatically updated.

```
// Placed DataBindingClasses in the Library
import mx.data.binding.*;
var src = new EndPoint();
src.component = src_txt;
src.property = "text";
src.event = "focusOut";

var dest = new EndPoint();
dest.component = dest_txt;
dest.property = "text"
new Binding(src, dest);
```

What the Sam Hill??

What's going on here? Well, you can probably figure most of it out yourself. We import the data binding classes that make this code possible

```
import mx.data.binding.*;
```

Doing this allows us to create **EndPoints**. **EndPoints** are objects that know about a component: what it is, which property to look at, and what event triggers the data binding to update the destination **EndPoint**.

Now, let's create the actual `EndPoints`:

```
var src = new EndPoint();
var dest = new EndPoint();
```

Yeah, I know I'm going out of order here. You can keep up—I have faith in your big brain.

Now that we created `EndPoint` objects, we need to point them at something. First, the source `EndPoint`:

```
src.component = src_txt;
src.property = "text";
src.event = "focusOut";
```

First, we point at the component `src_txt`. Then, we set which property we care about. In this case, it's **text**, which makes sense, since this is a text field. If it was a radio button or drop-down, we'd probably care more about the **data** property.

Also, since this is the `EndPoint` used for the source, we set an event that triggers the data binding—in this case, `focusOut`. We could also use `change`, which would then update the destination text field every time a character changed.

Now it's time to set the destination:

```
dest.component = dest_txt;
dest.property = "text"
```

Pretty simple, eh? We identify the component that will change and the property that will be affected. Notice that we didn't bother with an event. Why should we? We don't care what the destination field does. As far as data binding is concerned, the destination component's only purpose in life is to receive data.

Finally, we make the data binding official and tell ActionScript which is the source and which is the destination.

```
new Binding(src, dest);
```

That's it! Arr, ye data be bound.

Getting Deeper

What things can be endpoints? Endpoints can be a constant value, a component property, or a certain field of a component property. It has to be something from which you can get data or to which you can assign data. (I know that sounds obvious, but keep it in mind anyway. Trust me.)

Index

informIT

YOUR GUIDE TO IT REFERENCE

Articles

Keep your edge with thousands of free articles, in-depth features, interviews, and IT reference recommendations – all written by experts you know and trust.

Online Books

Answers in an instant from **InformIT Online Book's** 600+ fully searchable on line books. For a limited time, you can get your first 14 days **free**.

Safari
POWERED BY
TECH BOOKS ONLINE®

Catalog

Review online sample chapters, author biographies and customer rankings and choose exactly the right book from a selection of over 5,000 titles.

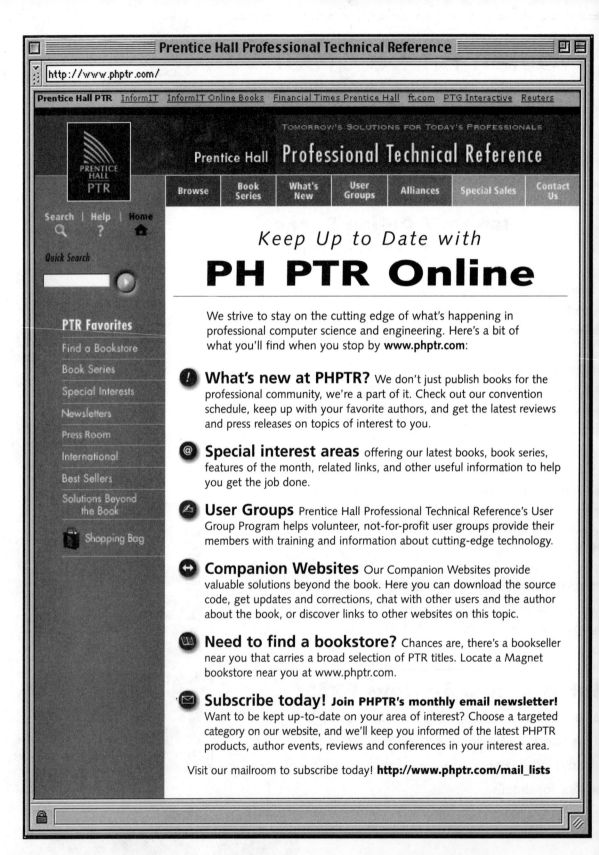